PRANAYAMA

The present book introduces us intelligently to the basic breathing practices and describes the fundamental aspects of their psycho-physiology. This is meant for the people who are following a hectic life in the world of constant and fast changing surroundings. This will help to experience with their own breath consciously to bring a harmonious balance in their constitution of the body, mind and soul and thereby getting tranquility, inner satisfaction and confidence in their life.

This may prove panacea to people who are weary of their restless activities and longing for inner peace, an inborn desire of the soul, a spiritual heritage of human beings. Further it may help to build a bridge between the internal and external life to maintain balance and harmony in between positive and negative aspects of life.

My Guru Sri Bishnu Charan Ghosh (1903-1970)
Master of Yoga and Physical Culture
Younger brother of Paramahansa Yogananda

Note: In India since ages it was a ritual tradition for Yogis to meditate sitting on tiger skins to achieve the mystical power, before the awareness on extinction of tiger appeared in human consciousness. Nowadays mostly the deerskins are used for meditation and other ritual purposes.

PRANAYAMA

A Conscious Way of Breathing

RANJIT SEN GUPTA

New Age Books

ISBN: 81-7822-083-0

Second Revised Edition: Delhi, 2005
First Edition: 2003

© 2000 by R. Sen Gupta
(registered with US of Copyright Office
Registration No. Txu 1-000-932)

Published by
NEW AGE BOOKS
A-44 Naraina Phase-I
New Delhi-110 028 (INDIA)
Email: nab@vsnl.in
Website: www.newagebooksindia.com

Printed in India
at Shri Jainendra Press
A-45 Naraina Phase-I New Delhi-110 028

Dedicated to

My Guru late Sri Bishnu Charan Ghosh
and
my dear father late Sri Sachindra Mohan Sen Gupta.
They both gave me the insight in Yoga and
formed my character. Their loving presence was
my ideal and that will remain for ever.

Foreword*

Pranayama is the conscious perception and guidance of life energies which unfold self in complex form in the psycho-physical system of all living beings. Pranayama is thus more than a system of breath control. Pranayama has several aspects, in the coarse material body and in the fine material body, directly perceptible ones and more subtly hidden ones. Prana manifests itself in body movements, in the metabolism, in sexuality and in all conscious procedures, and shows itself particularly clearly in the act of breathing. All great cultural traditions of mankind have amassed a fund of experimental knowledge of correlations between body and soul particularly evident in the function of breathing. The act of breathing is therefore the easiest accessible connecting link between vegetative functions and mentally guided procedures, because it is involved in both spheres: we breathe as long as we live – in fact, life means breath. Even when we are unconscious, we continue to breathe. However, at the same time the act of breathing can also be subdued under conscious perception and guidance. Thus, the entire psycho-physical system, including the subconscious activities, can be brought into balance and harmony by consciously directed way of breathing. Pranayama is the central practice of Yoga.

Yoga is a philosophy of life. It is a matter of perfect practice and co-ordination of three levels of activity: Physical, psychic and material, with the key to success being the exact coordinated practice of these three levels. This has an effect on one's philosophy of life. The dualism between body and mind or even the reducing of the human being on the level of physiologically explainable and mechanically interpreted procedures do correspond neither with the theory nor with the practical experiences of Yoga. The aim is to influence the physical level by mental processes (concentration,

---

* Original text in German translated by the author.

attentiveness), which in turn stabilize the mind. Thus with the mind resting in absolute tranquility, it is no longer subjected to the stimuli previously provided by the senses. The mind becomes "transparent", becomes absorbed in itself and reaches a self-knowledge which would not be possible in our general consciousness, when we are busy reacting sensual stimuli or thinking about past experiences. This is where the function of breathing plays a crucial role. By careful and exactly co-ordinated ways of breathing we release psycho-physical reactions, which prove man to be a continuance of body and mind. Physical and mental imbalances can thus be overcome and be integrated and the person can be healed in mind and body.

Nowadays in the West, too, there are authentic Yoga teachers and excellent courses and a host of literature available which allows to go on the path of Yoga in an acceptable way that suits the western ways of life. The presented book introduces us intelligently to the basic breathing practices and describes the fundamental aspects of their psycho-physiology. With thanks deserving accuracy the author provides the necessary core information. It is true that Pranayama can only be achieved through practical training under the guidance of a competent teacher. However, this written text presents a necessary first orientation and it will also prove to be perpetual helpful to the advanced students on the way to practice.

Munich, in November 2001   **Michael von Brück**

Preface to the Second Edition

This book brings to the reader the age-old techniques of Pranayama.

It is a belief in yoga that the length of one's life is measured by the destined number of breathing one does in one's life period and not just by years or days. In Pranayama then one can diminish the breath frequency (number of breath done per minute) and that causes the stretching of the life span.

Yogis achieve the peace of mind by controlling their breath through Pranayama practice.

By regular practice of Pranayama we achieve a deep consciousness of our own breath, our constant companion of us from birth to death. This breath consciousness shall then become one of the important tasks in our life, because a pure breath keeps the physical and mental status of our life on a divine path. On the contrary the impurity of breath brings many life's aspects in unbalanced conditions.

Men act nobler and purer when through breath consciousness they realize that the breath in a spiritual sense is the breath of God and that makes life divine. Thus we communicate through our breath with our inner most being *"Atma"*, the manifestation of the divine being in us (Kriya Yoga). Thus spiritual attunement begins with breath consciousness.

Through breath consciousness we can go deep within us and find our own midst and that brings a rhythmic balance in our daily life.

This awareness of breath rhythm brings mental balance and harmony, creating one's own magnetism. The vibration of the magnetism gives men an amiable and trusty appearance. So the breath consciousness does not allow disharmony in life. Mastering the breath rhythm one can master the inner status of mind and that activates also the power of self control.

Constant attention to our breath makes us conscious of Prana, the divine life energy. Prana also means soul so with pure breath we nourish our soul.

Intentionally I have tried to avoid as much as possible to use Sanskrit phrases for my book easy accessible to all readers.

Mistakes in the first edition have now been corrected in this edition.

Also the photos of the figures 15 to 22 of the first edition are now replaced by better photos in the second edition.

Ranjit Sen Gupta

Preface to the First Edition

Several publications are to be found in the book market on the subject Yoga with Pranayama as appendix, the age-old Indian way of Yoga initiated breathing process but very few books on Pranayama as main subject. What is then the purpose of publishing this book on the subject Pranayama? The answer is that each author writes his own way of approach to the same subject for the readers and the author here wants to put emphasis especially on the subject of Pranayama, the conscious way of breathing. By that readers have the possibility to get a wide range of view to find their own personal engagements to this subject.

This book is composed to reach those readers living in the modern world of high-tech environment and life-style, especially in the West and searching for a soothing opposite pole to the external hectic life in the world of constant and fast changing surroundings to live an inner life in balance and harmony. When we are in a condition of stress, hectic and irritation causing nervousness, then our breath becomes flat and faster. In this state a deep and steady breathing, consciously done for at least few minutes, brings release in the said condition. Simultaneously the physical parts of the body also find a relaxation. This is a simple act of Pranayama. Through directed breathing practice one finds back to the origin of own balanced life in inner happiness and self-control.

Verily most people of today's world of technology keep themselves extremely engaged in restless activities of their external life, as in profession, in free time disposition and so on. Thereby they are not any more aware of the natural longing for inner life. Though longing for inner life is an inborn desire of the soul, a spiritual heritage of human beings, yet generally this part of life remains in us quite folded or neglected, either out of unconsciousness or willingly to avoid confrontation with the own self and by that not to face the own inner being. But this confrontation is needed for them who want to build a bridge between the internal and external life, which will be then the path of finding balance and harmony in between positive and negative aspects of life. Only in deep meditation one is able to face the confrontation with self to become detached from external bondage. To reach the state of deep meditation we need to prepare ourselves step by step, getting free from outer influences and excitements, becoming calm and quiet in body and mind, increasing the intensity grade of concentration.

What most people consider as meditation, is in reality concentration. Pure form of meditation brings us freedom from the firm hold of lower instinct and mind. This transcends all our anxiousness, desire, eagerness and negative emotions to create a new positive channel in our mind and to eliminate the destructive part[1].

Hence the concentration process is the first step in the advancement towards the absolute state of meditation. Knowledge has been gained by the concentration power of the mind, said Swami Vivekananda[2].

Thus Pranayama is the key to the concentration process. Because one needs to follow the various breathing rhythms and timing, mind's perceptivity, as well as the physiological aspects of the body and mind, in the process of practicing Pranayama. Pranayama is not only a key to the concentration process but also keeps our body and mind spiritually and physically regenerated and healthy. Breathing has two aspects in our life. One is the usual breathing to keep our life alive, a biological function of the body. The other is the Pranayama, an initiated breathing path which, going through intensive and advanced practices, leads ultimately to an absolute state of pure meditation for higher spiritual consciousness.

Through this book I want to reach those, who wants to experience their own breath consciously to bring a harmonious balance in their constitution of the body, mind and soul and thereby to find the tranquility, inner satisfaction and confidence in their life.

As it would be appropriate here to know also the physiological aspects of breath in our body, so chapter I begins with the relevant introduction in respiration physiology, followed by chapters on Pranayama.

Ranjit Sen Gupta

---

1. Quotation: Swami Vishnu Devananda.
2. Raja Yoga, Swami Vivekananda.

Acknowledgement

My first grateful thanks go to my dear wife Karima for her constant support in my writing this book. It was her repeated encouragement that inspired me to write this book.

I am deeply thankful to Mrs. Ana Perez-Chisti, Ph.D., professor of Religion and Philosophy at Naropa University-Oakland Campus and at the University of Creation Spirituality in Oakland, California, USA, who spent lot of hours in her friendly engagement in proofing and correcting the English language of the book with worthy advices, besides her immense work in the university, in social work and especially in her leading Sufi activities.

In a same way I am very grateful to Dr. Michael von Brück, professor of Religious Science, University of Munich, Germany, Yoga and Zen Teacher in Germany, India and USA, for his profound foreword to my book.

It is my postmortem gratefulness to my co-disciple late Dr. Gouri Shankar Mukherjee, a great Yogi, whose few Yoga postured photos I have used in my book.

My thanks go also to Mrs. Sandra Schenk, a yoga disciple, who accepted to sit before my camera for explaining photos, which are used in this book.

Also I thank my friend and physician Dr. med. Dieter Bernoulli, who proved the correctness of the contents of the first chapter of this book.

Ranjit Sen Gupta

Contents

Chapter VI

Chapter VII

List of Figures and Charts

---

* All postures 15 to 22b by Sandra Schenk

24. Shavasana (Posture by late Dr. G. S. Mukherjee).
25. Timing for alternating Pranayama practice Course-3.
26. Functional diagram of intermitting Pranayama.
27. Chakra centers front view, vitality level of spiritual consciousness (at the permission of Aurum-Westermann Verlag, Braunschweig, Germany, "Das grosse illustrierte Yoga Buch" by Swami Vishnu Devananda).
28. Chakra centers side view (at the courtesy of the German magazine Esotera, July 1999).
29. Daily Pranayama program after the end of 120 weeks training.
30. Lesson-1   Training chart.
31. Lesson-2   Training chart.
32. Lesson-3   Training chart.
33. Lesson-4   Training chart.
34. Lesson-5   Training chart.
35. Lesson-6   Training chart.
36. Lesson-7   Training chart.
37. Lesson-8   Training chart.
38. Lesson-9   Training chart.
39. Lesson-10   Training chart.

I

Physiology of Breathing

People of modern age keep themselves quite engaged in several forms of sport activities for their physical fitness; like jogging, swimming, aerobic, several kinds of games etc. By that they are naturally exposed to higher rate of breathing than normal. Now the question in respect to this book may arise: what are the differences between the breathing function of an exercising person in above mentioned sport arts and that of a person practicing Pranayama? We will find the answer of this question during the evolution of following passages.

This chapter shall therefore explain first the basic science of Respiratory Physiology, so far it is relevant to the subject of this book and then gradually switches over to the essence of Pranayama.

I-1 Respiratory Physiology

This is a science that deals with the respiratory processes and functions in a living body. The basal function here is the adequate adjusting exchange of O_2 and CO_2 between the environment and the alveolus according to the demand of O_2 uptake to transform venous blood into the arterial blood and that of CO_2 discharge out of body's metabolism. Alveolus are the numerous blind sacs in the end of an extremely complex system of our lungs, where the gas exchange actually takes place. The lung is an active metabolic organ and regulates various important biological substances, besides some other chemical functions.

There are two kinds of respiration, internal and external. The internal respiration is a subject of biochemistry, a process of metabolizing nourishing stuffs. Therefore, this subject will not be followed here further. The external respiration is the subject of this chapter. It briefly deals with the physiology of fundamental gas exchange in various lung volumes and capacities, of breathing patterns; of the airways; of the dynamics of the breathing mechanism and of the neural control system in breath regulation. At the end of this chapter a brief outline will be given between breath function in exercise and in Pranayama, supported by a comparing table.

I-2 Lung Volumes and Capacities

Clinically the lung volumes and capacities are divided in eight functional components, as shown in figure 1.

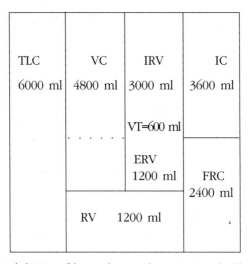

Figure 1 Related division of lung volume and capacity in a healthy young man.

Total Lung Capacity (TLC) =VC + RV or IC + FRC

This is the maximum volume of gas contained in the lung after total inspiration.

Vital Capacity (VC) = IRV + V_T + ERV or IC + ERV

VC is the maximum volume of air which can be theoretically exhaled (down to the level of RV) after deepest possible inhalation. But in practice VC comes down mostly up to the level of ERV (see dot line) at our normal state of breathing.

Residual Volume (RV): This is the gas volume that remains in the lung at point VC. This volume cannot be exhaled in life time. RV is approximately 20% of TLC at mid-age.

Functional Residual Capacity (FRC) = ERV + RV

This is the remaining gas volume at which point the change of respiratory period is activated during normal breathing. As normally the exhalation does not come down to RV level (see part VC), so the exhalation is actually up to the mark line of FRC. At this point lungs and chest wall are elastically balanced and the respiratory system is in an equilibrium volume. FRC is about 40% of the TLC.

Inspiratory Capacity (IC) = IRV + V_T

IC is a maximum possible inhalation, activated from FRC position. Practically most or many people inhale much less volume than the available capacity during each normal breath, known as flat and short breathing, out of insufficient expansion of chest wall and diaphragm.

Tidal Volume (V_T): This is the volume being inhaled normally at each breath in rest condition, which is quite less than IC. The V_T can be increased more efficiently to utilize IRV by voluntary efforts, inhaling more deeply rather than exhaling deeply.

Inspiratory Reserve Volume (IRV): Available reserve volume to increase V_T to match full IC, see above.

Expiratory Reserve Volume (ERV): A considerable reserve volume that remains in the lungs after normal exhalation and this can be utilized through voluntary breathing technique.

The voluntary increase of V_T causes fluctuations in IRV and ERV during the ventilation process of respective inhalation and exhalation. To make these features more clear to the readers, certain values in ml are put to each division. The ranges of values differ basing on the factors age, sex, physical structures and condition, environment, etc. A value of 6000 ml as total lung capacity is being generally taken as typical for a normal healthy person at rest. The tidal volume figures normally between 500 and 600 ml at each breath. In this case V_T is taken as 600 ml which is usually 10% of TLC. Out of 600 ml V_T per breath about 450 ml enters the alveolus, the place of gas exchange in the lungs, and the rest 150 ml remains in the airway, so called dead space. Explanation of dead space is not given here, because there is no intention here to go deep into the medical science. The gas flow increases parallel to the metabolic rate of increase, as in case of exercise or heavy work. The further values are:

- ERV is double than that of V_T = 1200 ml

- RV is same as ERV = 1200 ml
- IRV is as much as 3000 ml., a reserve volume to increase V_T five times more to match maximal IC
- IC is then obviously the sum of IRV and V_T = 3600 ml
- FRC is 40% of TLC = 2400 ml, as previously mentioned in the definition of FRC
- VC is then the sum of IRV, V_T and ERV or IC and ERV = 4800 ml, see previous definition of VC

Thus the tidal volume can be expanded up to five tidal volumes more by voluntary inhalation to meet the full IC and this is being physically attuned during Pranayama practices. It is clear from figure 1 that IC can never be equal to VC by increasing V_T to maximum. Though the exhaling volume could reach theoretically the full VC, but in reality it does not. The reason of this difference lies in medical details of the energy efficiency balance of the lungs and therefore will not be further followed up here. It is also to be noted here that lung volume and its subdivisions change by the growing age. FRC increases at cost of decreased IC and RV at a lesser degree due to elasticity loss of lung recoil. The chest mobility decreases due to the growing stiffness of the thoracic cage. But by keeping a regular breathing practice, say Pranayama, one can be resistant against the said elasticity loss at prolonged age.

I-3 Breathing Patterns

The alternating gas exchange between lungs and environment through constant respiration, as we know, is defined as breathing. And the breathing patterns depend upon the ventilation rate. That is the total quantity of air exchange per unit of time and varies according to particular patterns of breathing. The ventilation rate is calculated by multiplying V_T the tidal volume and breathing frequency (f), the number of breath done per minute. Thus, ventilation rate is V_T ´ (f) = litre per minute. It can be mentioned here without going deep into the subject, that breathing patterns effect the distribution and disposition site of inhaled particles, suspended aerosol in air, such as smoke particles in different parts of the lungs.

There are several breathing patterns, standard and abnormal which are well classified in medical science, but all of them are not relevant to the purpose of this book. Therefore, two primary autonomic patterns and a voluntary pattern will be shortly described below. By that readers can have some insight in their regular breathing arts which they normally do unconsciously, except medical oriented persons.

Eupnea Pattern

This is what we in unawareness usually breathe when the ventilation rate is in a match with the metabolic demand of the body at rest. In this case (f) is between 13 to 17 breaths per minute and V_T is about 600 ml (see figure 1). Correctly, V_T (Tidal Volume) is given in ml BTPS. BTPS means at body temperature, pressure and saturated with water vapor at that temperature, effecting the V_T value. To not make the subject more complicated the BTPS definition in detail is left out here. Thus, the ventilation rate of this pattern is about 7.8 l/min., accepting (f) = 13 as an average value.

Hyperpnea Pattern

In this pattern, the ventilation rate is higher than in the case of Eupnea pattern to match the higher metabolic demand as in case of muscular exercise where both V_T and f are naturally increased. It is known medically that increase of ventilation during exercise stays directly in proportion to the rate of performance to a certain point. Beyond this point the increase in ventilation becomes disproportionate to discharge excess CO_2. The maximum performance abilities during exercise are being regulated by breathing in ideal case, but unfortunately that does not happen always and is the cause of several breathing problems such as hyperventilation, ventilation that exceeds metabolic demands, a response to heavy exercise as example. Whereby in case of Pranayama V_T can be voluntarily increased as much as upto full IC without physical strain and (f) is thereby decreased as much as 50 to 60% of the normal state, resulting in lower ventilation rate and sure absence of hyperventilation.

Breath Holding

In this pattern the respiratory movements are being voluntarily ceased. In some cases this occurs even automatically when the body's receptors (upper airway, etc.) provide sensation to protect against inhaling undesired agents, like odd smells, unfiltered smoke outlet of a chimney, etc. that are cumulated in air. Also in several occasions in our daily life we hold breath consciously or unconsciously for certain occasions, as in case of sudden injury, pain, bowel movements, coughing, lifting heavy weight, while diving and during some swimming style and so on. Musicians like singers, wind instrument players learn to control subglottal pressure to produce steady sound notes.

The limit (breakpoint) of a hold period, a contest between will and sensation, depends much upon the level of CO_2 tolerance,

Figure 2 Performance of breath-holding.

personal physical abilities, motivation and self-discipline. For prolonged breath holding, a large initial lung volume is needed and as well as the lowering down of metabolic rate, a result of voluntary prior hyperventilation. Thus moderate deep breathing (hyperventilation) for some minutes remarkably lower down the CO_2 level, allowing space for uptake of metabolically produced CO_2 during subsequent breath-holding.

This was also practiced by the writer during his young age performance in passing over a 3 ton weighing elephant over his chest in laying down position, as depicted in figure 2.

During the period of breath holding the lung volume decreases as well as the chest wall volume decreases in same proportion, because lungs and chest wall moves as a unit. By that intrathoracic pressure increases and the air in the lung is trapped and pressurized. This stabilizes the chest wall and gives physical resistant capacity to hold the heavy weight load for a few seconds. Obviously it is to be mentioned here that the major function in this case was the breath-holding with quite less inhaled air to adjust the reduced lung volume out of the decreased dimension of thoracic cage due to the external weight pressure. Besides this also a strong and elastic physical structure, long years of yoga practice combined with body building, were also essential for this act.

Longer breath-holding at a certain stage is subjected to the breakpoint as mentioned before, beyond which rebreathing is inevitably needed. A protective function to avoid unconsciousness. More specific passages on this subject are to be found in several medical publications.

Also in medicine, breath retaining techniques are used on patients for rehabilitation and also that what we commonly experience when the doctor asks for breath-holding during a heart check or so. Although the conscious breath-holding maneuvers are helpful and practiced in many circumstances, yet they should be avoided by people with lung disabilities like asthma, hypertension and so on.

Consequently, by practicing breath-holding, as it is often done in Pranayama, one can sensibly increase one's own resistance capacities, will power, self-discipline, neutralizing ability in stress situation, strength accumulation and spiritual attuning capacity. We will come back in later chapters on the subject of spiritual attunement.

In closing this paragraph of breathing patterns we shall be aware of the importance of breathing training (besides all its physiological aspects) is to bring harmony and balance between positive and negative aspects in our daily life, independent of any particular breathing patterns (except patterns out of medical cause) which have a relevant relation with Pranayama practice. Because breathing control teaches us indirectly to have control over our mind. It is or should be the natural ability of human beings to control his breathing in consciousness.

I-4 Airways

All air passages, the turbinate, the pharynx, the larynx, the extrathoracic portion of the trachea, etc., transmitting respiratory

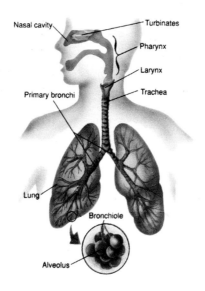

Figure 3   The anatomy of the respiratory system.

stream between the environment and down to the alveolus through the body's respiratory gateways; the nose and the mouth are being defined as airways, as shown in figure 3. During spontaneous breathing the airways actively deflate or constrict at corresponding inhalation and exhalation according to the respective increase and decrease of airway calibers. Hence, the airflow rate is considerably affected by an even small decrease in airway calibers and that widely increases airway resistance. Such resistance occurs out of physiological disorder or any kind of undesired or desired (in a certain Pranayama process) external influences and that cause for ventilatory disorder.

In Pranayama practices, the airway resistance is intentionally produced under precise control of flow rate in respiration cycle. This is done to attain a conscious breathing practice as well as to maintain airway hygiene. Details of such breathing control methods will be found in later chapters.

The vital part of the respiratory tract is the upper airway. The nose with turbinate, the mouth, the pharynx and larynx and part of trachea build the upper airway. Here we will concern ourselves mainly with the role of nose and mouth in the breathing process.

The remaining part of the airways will not be considered here and shall be kept in the domain of medical science.

With its mucous membranes, receptors, branches of nerves and turbinate the nose is very perfectly designed by nature to take up the primary breathing function. Thus, inhaling air is broadly modified by humidification and warmed up due to swirl function through turbinate (irregular surface). Also dust and other particles adhere to the nasal mucous as turbinate churn the air. This minimizes irritation and respiratory infection and differentiates the smell quality to protect airways from possible malfunction. These are the foremost advantages of nose breathing. The mouth breathing takes up the secondary respiration function when the exceed demand of air can not be satisfactorily drawn through the nose as in case of extreme athletic efforts or at nasal congestion such as by catching cold or out of medical cause. In all such unusual conditions respiratory muscles automatically force to switch over from nose to mouth breathing.

By mouth breathing the breathing capacity is corresponding negatively influenced as the oral passage is wider than the nasal passage and there is the absence of turbinate causing inappropriate air resistance. The degree to which this becomes true depends upon the variable position of one's jaws, tongue, lips, and palate. Also undesired problems appear in areas like neck and nose, when mouth breathing becomes a regularity.

It is also natural that the air stream does not flow always through both nostrils simultaneously but changes the path periodically from one to the other nostril. This alternation takes place in average intervals of 2 to 3 hours, which can be observed by self time to time. Different physiological, psychic and environmental perceptions cause such alterations.

Knowing these principal functions of nose and mouth breathing, Pranayama processes use several techniques during breathing to direct the rate and art of air stream mainly through the nostril. Hence, conducting of such breathing technique asks for conscious attentiveness.

Only few physiological studies and investigations have been made about the respiratory role of the nasal afferent (sensory nerve) to profoundly confirm the nasal receptor's functions. But the age old Pranayama philosophy strongly believes on spiritual radiation carried by the nasal afferent.

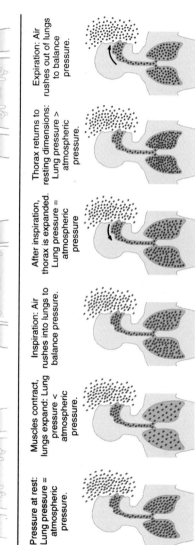

Figure 4 The process of inspiration and expiration, showing how movement of the ribs and diaphragm can increase and decrease the size of the thorax. (a) The dimensions of the lungs and the thoracic cage increase during inspiration forming a negative pressure that draws air into the lungs. (b) During expiration the lung volume decreases thereby forcing air out of the lungs.

a

At Rest

Inspiration

Thorax is expanded from inspiration.

Expiration

Ribs and sternum return downward, diaphragm relaxes and is pushed upward, and lung tissue recoils.

Sternum
Ribs
Diaphragm

b

Pressure at rest: Lung pressure = atmospheric pressure.

Muscles contract, lungs expand: Lung pressure < atmospheric pressure.

Inspiration: Air rushes into lungs to balance pressure.

After inspiration, thorax is expanded. Lung pressure = atmospheric pressure

Thorax returns to resting dimensions: Lung pressure > atmospheric pressure.

Expiration: Air rushes out of lungs to balance pressure.

I-5 Dynamics of Breathing Mechanism

A smooth change over from inhalation to exhalation over an unnoticed fraction of a pause between the two breaths is defined as breathing cycle. During each cycle there is a change in lungs and thorax which is defined as the dynamics of the breathing mechanism. The dynamics of inspiration and expiration are shown in figure 4.

The diaphragm and the external intercostal muscle (muscles between the ribs) are involved during inhalation as an active process. So then the inhalation is an active process, whereas the exhalation is usually a passive function involving the relaxation of the inspiratory muscles and natural elastic recoil of the lung tissues at normal resting breathing. But during forced (as in case of Pranayama) or labored breath, exhalation becomes more active, assisted by the involved muscle activities of the thorax region.

In three directions—lateral, anterior-posterior (a-p) and vertical, the thorax volume can be increased during inhalation process, as depicted in figure 4. It can be noted here that just the lateral and a-p movements bring together normally a change in volume which is as much as 40% of total lung volume, depending on the sitting, standing or laying position of the body.

Movement in lateral (lower chest) direction is when the ribs swing up and out, much like the movements of the bucket handle. Movement in a-p (upper chest) directions is when the sternum swings up and forward, much like the movements of a water pump handle. At the same time movement in vertical direction is when the diaphragm contracts, flattening down towards the abdomen, much like the movements of a bicycle pump. The simultaneous movement of all these three directions allows the lung to expand and stretch best during inspiration because the increased thorax dimension creates enough place for that, as shown in figure 4 a.

The expiration is accomplished when the aforesaid movements are in opposite direction. The diaphragm relaxes and returns to its normal upward, arched position. The external intercostal muscles relax, causing the ribs and sternum lower back into their resting position. Then the elastic nature of the lung tissues causes it to recoil to its resting size, as shown in figure 4 b.

Normally, we do not adapt or are conscious of this three-directive simultaneous breathing form in our normal breathing cycles. What we do mostly is a kind of short and flat breathing, as mentioned before. It is also observed when one is asked for a deep breathing, one then lifts the shoulders up during inhaling, and there is the absence of three-directive breathing. This way of breathing has also a massaging effect due to better blood circulation on abdominal viscera.

This three-directive simultaneous breathing is being practiced for centuries by the yogis in the Pranayama process and is defined as yoga-breathing. The definition of yoga-breathing will therefore be used for all arts of Pranayama practice in later chapters. This part may then be reviewed as necessary.

I-6 Neural Regulation of Breathing Cycle.

All previous paragraphs have dealt with several functions and movements in breathing cycles. To carry out these movements respiratory muscle coordination is needed. These coordinating activities are generated by the medullary neurons accumulated in the respiratory center. Though the medulla is isolated from the rest of the brain, above the level where it enters, yet the medullary center conducts the muscle movements for breathing. Thus, the breathing rhythm is generated in the lower brain stem. Hence, we can clearly realize that respiratory muscles can not move without the action of neural systems. Thus, the neural systems keep the breathing cycle in function for regular air exchange. The respiratory center is placed in the medulla and pons, a part of the Central Nervous System, called CNS. The CNS regulation of the cardiovascular system, based in the brain stem, is mainly an autonomous function and does not accept voluntary control.

The respiration regulating system being also an autonomous function acting over nerve currents responds to varieties of informations created by physiological activities and environments and thus reflex action modifies our usual breathing to the best of our demand. It is self active when we are in sleep or when we are unaware of our breathing cycles, while we are awake. Yet one is able to override voluntarily this autonomous process for a certain period and purpose when respiratory muscle movements are used to modify breathing (rapid, slow, precious) during singing, playing wind instruments, and guided skilled breathing plus breath-holding in Pranayama courses. But at a certain level, such as at the breakpoint of breath-holding, the automatic regulation system overrides again the voluntary acts, a protective function of respiratory physiology. Therefore, one shall be essentially conscious of this level of crossing over the breakpoint of voluntary longer breath-hold to avoid any discomfort or harm to the body by overdoing.

Through the neural regulation system our breathing reflects our emotional state in association with mental imagination. The antici-pation of activities, exciting or soothing, increase or smooth down the ventilation rate before such activity actually begins. For example, anxiety causes hyperventilation whereas by just thinking of medi-tation the respiration becomes quiet. This shows that our mind power has an intensive influence in the neural regulation system. Therefore Pranayama, the conscious way of breathing control, in the language of physiology which can be called as a skilled voluntary breathing maneuver, develops simultaneously also the sensory mind power and thus Pranayama practice becomes also an interac-tive part of the neural regulation system of respiration.

There are several components of the nervous system CNS, functionally organized to carry out movements, as shown in figure 5. Purposely I will not go deep into the complexity of the nervous system, to not to expand this subject. However, a few major components of CNS are being shortly explained here for the relative understanding for the readers in respect to following Pranayama processes.

The CNS is composed of brain and spinal chord. More than 100 billion neurons are housed in CNS. Here we find the affinity between the 100 billion neurons and the "Sahasrara Chakra", the thousand petals lotus at the top of the head, which is the highest consciousness center as described by ancient Yogis on the path of Kundalini. The brain stem is one of the four major divisions of the brain and is composed of the midbrain, the pons and the medulla oblongata. Medulla oblongata connects the spinal chord to the brain. The spinal chord carries both sensory and motor fibers between the brain and the periphery.

The Brain Stem

All sensory and motor nerves pass through the brain stem as they relay information between the brain and the spinal chord.

The Spinal Chord

This is composed of tracts of nerve fibers that allow two-way conduction of nerve impulses. The sensory fibers (afferent impulse, see figure 5) carry signals from sensory receptors, such as those in the muscles and joints, to the upper level of the CNS. Motor fibers (efferent impulse, see figure 5) carry neural signals from the brain and upper spinal chord down to end organs, muscles and glands. In advanced stage of Pranayama practice, interpreting Chakra Meditation we will find how the affinity of these two afferent and efferent nerve current influence in our breath flow.

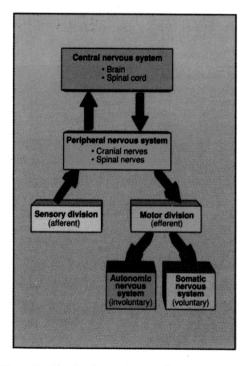

Figure 5   Functional organization of nervous system.

Peripheral Nervous System (PNS)

PNS consists of cranial and spinal nerves, functions as a terminal to communicate in and out information between afferent-efferent signals (sensory and motor division) and CNS.

Sensory (afferent) neurons send information via sensory receptors over PNS to CNS. Thus, the CNS is constantly aware of our current condition of our entire body and mind. Sensory receptors receive information originated in several areas of our body's and mind's circles. Some of these areas are the organs of special senses, like taste, touch, smell, hearing and vision. The senses of vision play a very subtle role in advanced Pranayama practice.

Motor (efferent) neurons carry responding actions out to our body and mind, that have been received by CNS and after CNS has processed the received information from the sensory nerves.

To conclude the nervous system as explained here, a short information on the Autonomic Nervous System (ANS) is given in the followings. The ANS, a part of the motor division of PNS, controls the body's involuntary internal functions; such as respiration during sleep. The ANS includes two major systems: the Sympathetic Nervous System (SNS) and the Parasympathetic Nervous System (PSNS).

The SNS prepares our body to face situations, created out of awareness or excitation, etc. resulting in a so-called fight or fly action. The PSNS is our body's housekeeping system, for example conservation of energy. This system is more active when we are calm and quiet and at rest. Though these two systems oppose each other yet they always function together.

Pranayama practices in combination with meditation (concentration) tune our body and mind to create calmness in us and obviously that has a great influence on PSNS to mould our body and mind towards harmonious and steady "Housekeeping".

In our daily awake life we do not give conscious attention to our breath. But we can become attentive and conscious of our breathing and by that change is created in afferent impulse. So the anticipation of doing Pranayama creates that afferent sensitive information in our mind, which causes us to become calm.

This CNS composition has shown us that our spinal chord is the most important transmission tube to carry afferent and efferent sensations. Therefore, in all Pranayama performances the spinal column shall be kept in an upright position. So to attain higher spiritual consciousness the great Yogis carry their divine energy through the spinal nerve currents to the fontanel, that energy that is created in their absolute pure meditation.

I-7 Difference in Breathing Aspects between Exercise and Pranayama

The prime difference between these two aspects of breathing can be described as: one is a passive process during exercising events, like several kinds of light or heavy sports and the other is an active process during Pranayama courses.

During exercising events the physical activities are first initiated. These cause for various physical changes, such as body's demand for more energy intake, demands for clearing off metabolic by-products and others. To compensate for these demands the body needs a higher rate of O_2 intake. That means a higher ventilation rate and an automatic function of neural breathing regulation system to maintain homeostasis to survive. Thus, an exercising person has no or very less voluntary control possibility to increase the tidal volume and breathing frequency (consult chapter I-2 if needed), as the ventilation rate becomes autonomous to meet physiological needs. Muscular performance creates multifaceted demands on the ventilatory control system. Regulation of ventilatory response to exercise is integrative and comprehensive. Hence, the breathing function here becomes passive. Besides that increased rate of respiration in exercising events causes for higher heart and pulse rate as well as for excitement and stress, especially in case of competitive events. Excitement and stress also put pressure on our nervous system.

Another aspect of breathing during exercise is that, this is absolutely a physical performance without having any spiritual background. There is also a decline in performance efficiencies at old age, after the fourth or fifth decade of life and such performances are mostly ceased at further aging. These views are not meant here to judge in any way the quality of these aspects but just to give the facts to show the difference with Pranayama.

The breathing methods in Pranayama differ in various points to the breathing performances mentioned above. Pranayama is practiced in a quiet atmosphere and at resting mood of our body and mind. Breathing is performed actively without a need of compensating any biophysical demand of the body as there is an absence of physical performances. It is a very conscious way of voluntary breathing performance with deep spiritual engagement, involving various rhythmic breathing patterns and frequencies. So the autonomic respiratory regulation system is here intentionally overridden. In this process, the respiration rate remains low resulting in a low heart and pulse rate, whereby the inspiratory tidal volume is well increased through long inhalation to the best utilization of inspiratory capacity. Thus, the Pranayama process can increase the tidal volume (see V_T in chapter I-2) more precisely than in normal cases and the breathing frequency is brought down to a relatively lower level, except in some special cases of Pranayama. The rhythmic way of Pranayama practice in meditative base creates no state of excitement or stress but brings calmness in the body's nervous system. Pranayama performances from early age do not or less decline the lung capacity at growing age. It is independent of the age factor for a normal healthy person, except in case of illness. Pranayama exercises bring intensive movements on respiratory muscles which increase the Vital Capacity (VC). Figure 6 shows in a comparing table the summarized aspects of differences between the events of exercise and Pranayama.

Aspects	Exercising Events	Pranayama
Breathing art	passive	active
Bio-physical demand	present	absent
Respiration rate	high	low
Breath control	autonomous	voluntary
Impact on nervous system	exciting	calming
Age factor	limited	nearly unlimited
Motivation	physical	physical and spiritual

Figure 6 Comparing table

Conclusion of Chapter

Descriptions that are given in this chapter intend to give a medical and scientific support to Pranayama practice and philosophy, which is deeply based on spiritual background. In the following chapters, we will find the elaborate descriptions on the process of Pranayama.

References

1. Allan H. Mines, Ph.D., *Respiratory Physiology,* Third Edition, Lippincott Williams and Wilkins Publishing Co., Philadelphia (Original Raven Press, New York, 1993).
2. Jerome A. Dempsey, Allan I. Pack, *Regulation of Breathing,* Second Edition, Marcel Dekker Inc, NY, 1995.
3. N. Balfour Slonim, M.D., Lyle H. Hamilton, Ph.D., *Respiratory Physiology,* Fifth Edition, The C.V. Mosby Co. St. Luis, Missouri, 1987.
4. Jack H. Wilmore, David. L. Costill, *Physiology of Sport and Exercise, Champaign,* IL, *Human Kinetics,* 1994 First Edition and 1999 Second Edition.

Credit Lines

Figure 1 Diagram at the courtesy of Allan H. Mines, Ph.D., 1993, *Respiratory Physiology*, 3rd Edition (Lippincott Williams and Wilkins, PA, former Raven Press, NY), Page 11.

Figure 2 Photo provided by the author.

Figures 3 & 5 Reprinted, by permission, from J.H. Wilmore & D.L. Costill, 1994, *Physiology of Sport and Exercise*, (Champaign, IL: *Human Kinetics*), pages 192 & 53.

Figure 4 Reprinted, by permission, from J.H. Wilmore & D.L. Costill, 1999, Physiology of Sport and Exercise, Second Edition. (Champaign, IL: *Human Kinetics*), page 248.

Figure 6 Table provided by the author.

II

Yoga - The Basis of Pranayama

The roots of Pranayama are based on the Yoga Science. Therefore, we will take first some brief steps in the teachings and philosophy of Yoga to get into the foundation of Pranayama. For more than centuries before Christ the great sage and philosopher of India *Patanjali* manifested first the science of Yoga. In his Yoga Sutra, he teaches the methods, how a Yogi can attain the stage of absolute consciousness to become one with the divine being by eliminating one's own egoistic self.

II-1 Path of Yoga

The Yoga Philosophy became first known to the West through Swami Vivekananda when he addressed at the Parliament of Religions in Chicago on 11th September, 1893. Later in 1920, Paramahansa Yogananda addressed to the International Congress of Religions in Boston. In the same year, he disseminates his world-wide teachings on India's ancient science of Yoga philosophy, the Kriya Yoga. This was the beginning of widely spreading of Yoga Culture in the West.

Now whenever we talk about Yoga in the West we mostly mean Yoga-Asanas, the several sitting and standing postures practiced in Hatha-Yoga. But Yoga Asanas are only a part of discipline in the vast Yoga Science, in Sanskrit Yoga Sastra. The principal purpose of Yoga Sastra is to enlighten progressively our latent conscious-ness, an inborn source of perception (mind, higher intellect and the real self) for all human beings, towards the path of divine realization in us, a spiritual path free of any limitation such as race or caste, or nation, the limitation that draws us back from any spiritual progress.

The Sanskrit word Yoga verbally means union or add together but its real meaning lies in a higher level. It is a spiritual union, transforming the folded "I" into an unfolded "I" to unite the higher self with the divine being. The word "I" has a two-fold meaning. One is the egoistic and the other lies in spiritual level which is impressively expressed in a Sanskrit verse of Brihadaranyaka Upanishad "Aham Satyam", which means "I am the truth", here I means the higher level of "I", called as Atman. Therefore, the unfoldment of "I" is a constant psychic and physical process in Yoga culture to make oneself free from the layers of bondage that is created in us out of our human ignorance. It is a process like peeling off onion skins till nothing exists than the absolute knowledge of truth. Then the individual self can unite with the higher self and that is Yoga, the revelation of absolute truth of "I am". To overcome our earthly ego, first we shall be aware that our individual consciousness is only part of the eternal consciousness. The Yoga brings the earthly consciousness to be one with the divine consciousness. The Yoga is also defined as harness. So all harnesses which create psychic burden in our life like animosity, anger, negative emotions, temptations, etc. are to be mastered through the path of discipline in Yoga. Yoga is again defined as yoking. According to Mahatma Gandhi, this is the yoking of all senses of our body, mind and soul towards the divinity by influencing all inner senses in us through the Yoga discipline. Yoga in the whole is a union of physiological and psychological aspects of human being.

The method of Yoga is the liberation of the soul through perfection, says Swami Vivekananda. And the perfection is achieved through the control of mind power. A controlled mind power has always a positive influence in us, whereas an uncontrolled mind causes for negative aspects in our life. In human being the power of mind, the capacities of higher perceptions are kept concealed by nature and they wait to be disclosed and manifested in life by our self. Through the conscious way of breathing practice Pranayama, an essential part of the Yoga teaching according to Patanjali, we learn to trace out our inner capacities to control our mind and lower egos and thus we take influence in our inner life stream to manifest in us the higher human value. By that we become aware of our own true beings, as well as we enlarge our consciousness to higher attunement and that creates a harmonious link between the three aspects of our life: body, mind and soul. Harmony in life creates peace and satisfaction in us.

The powers of the mind are like rays of light dissipated; when they are concentrated they illumine. This is our only means of knowledge, says Swami Vivekananda. He also writes that the perfected mind can be attached to all the organs simultaneously. It has the reflexive power of looking back into its own depths. This reflexive power is what the Yogi wants to attain; by concentrating the powers of the mind, and turning them inwards he seek to know what is happening inside. Therefore, the Pranayama and mind perception (both breath and mind are very subtle and fine matter) build together the energy field to achieve the higher consciousness.

The entire Raja-Yoga, one of the four Yoga disciplines, is based upon *Sankhya Philosophy. Sankhya Philosophy* explains how the origin of perception is generated in us. As defined by Swami Vivekananda in his book of Raja Yoga, the genesis of perception is the affections of external objects that are carried by the external senses (receptors) to their respective brain centers (CNS). This again transfers the affection to the mind and the mind to the determinative faculty. From this Purusha, the true light of inner being, the soul, the passionless self (Upanishad) receives the resulted perception. Next Purusha returns the received senses back, as it were, to the motor centers to effect our consciousness. Here we realize what a fine sensory receptor our mind is to carry out visions. In this place we may review the part of CNS in chapter I (figure 5) to realize how the mind sensation physiologically functions (afferent and efferent nerve currents) when we consciously pattern our breathing and tune our thoughts towards inner being through Pranayama practices. Of course, it is not possible to realize this subtle spiritual perception in us in a very short period, as it is often expected in the fast moving Western life, but after long years of intensive practice in deep humility this may reveal the inner being.

II-2 Classification of Yoga

Yoga is classified in four directions:

Raja Yoga: This is the path of observing the internal state of mind and by that mastering our mind capacity to find the ultimate truth of life through the Yoga methods of concentration and meditations.

Karma Yoga: This is the path to eliminate our negative egos through selfless deeds and service for humanity and by that realization of divinity.

Jnana Yoga: It is a path to uncover our inborn ignorance for higher knowledge about our true self and real nature, a divine being. Knowledge to find the real path in-between Maya and Illusion. Realization of supreme Unity.

Bhakti Yoga: It is a path for divine union through transcending our loving emotions in deep devotion. The spiritual realization through supreme devotion.

All these four directions fulfil the principal purpose of Yoga philosophy, as written before, each in their own way. Yet they are not contradictory to each other, rather they integrate the whole philosophy of Yoga to become the One. In this connection great Sri Swami Shivananda says, "that all four directions are not equally appropriate to all persons as each of the them possesses an individual character." Therefore, each person shall choose one out of the four directions as his or her main path according to their inclination to the said paths and the rest as supplements for his or her spiritual development towards inner life.

As in Raja-Yoga we will find the roots of Pranayama we shall go through some steps more in Raja Yoga. There are three other Yoga classifications which belong to Raja Yoga. They are Hatha Yoga, Kundalini Yoga (now a days both are well known in the West) and Mantra Yoga. See figure 7 for a quick glance in the branches of Raja Yoga.

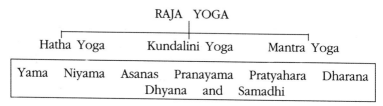

Figure 7   Raja Yoga and its three sub-Yoga arts
with their eight common basic disciplines of Yoga.

The eight-graded basic disciplines on the path of Yoga are commonly called in Sanskrit "Astanga Yoga" whereby "Asta" means eight and "anga" means part or step, verbally limb. All Yoga arts, specially Raja Yoga are based on these disciplines which are to be followed by all who want to follow the path of Yoga. These are the progressing steps of physical and mental preparation to reach the higher state of consciousness to the fulfillment of Raja-Yoga. Raja-Yoga means the king of Yoga and it is a path of sublimating the external and internal nature of us. In Hatha Yoga we approach Brahma by controlling the Prana, whereby in Raja Yoga the approach to Brahma is done by mind.

II-3 Eight Disciplines of Astanga Yoga

II-3.1 Yama (Controlling)
This is a part of moral and ethic teaching to keep away our all negative thoughts and deeds which cause unnecessary harm to all living beings. It strengthens the moral courage. It is a process of inner purification.

II-3.2 Niyama (Rules and Disciplines)
Here the rules and regulations are given to attain purity, self-control, satisfaction, to grow knowledge and to perform religious rituals. Ritual acts are very important in human life process. They have a deep positive influence in our psychic development. This keeps us pure in body and mind.

II-3.3 Asanas (Physical Postures)
These are the ways of tuning our body by figuring several forms of physical postures. These allow us to keep the physical elasticity of our body, correct figures and steadiness of our mind and create a future field for holding the longer meditation period.

II-3.4 Pranayama (Yogic Breathing Process)
An age-old conscious way of active breathing control practices, an important function of Yoga teaching. These practices give us physical and spiritual sustenance to guide our life-stream (*Prana*) efficiently. By that we gain influences in our life process for higher attitudes.

II-3.5 Pratyahara (Withdraw)
A discipline to retract from external senses and activities to get conceptions towards inner perceptions. Through this discipline we learn also to overcome our greediness in many objects we meet in life. Greediness puts stones on the path of inner life. In the present consume-oriented and egocentric world it is very difficult to keep oneself detached from the imposed temptation effecting from outside, more is in chapter VI.

II-3.6 Dharana (Conceived Concentration)

An act of concepted concentration in one point or an absolute attention to a performance for a certain object, holding the thoughts steady and undisturbed against unwanted influences. It is also the preparation for the next step, more is in chapter VI.

II-3.7 Dhyana (Meditation)

A state of meditation achieved after a long and permanent practice of Dharana, more is in chapter VI.

II-3.8 Samadhi (Union with the Absolute)

This is the state of mind when the perfect concentration is transformed in a super-consciousness which goes beyond the limits of reason. The mind is then brought in a higher state of vibration to attain absolute spiritual realization in immersed meditation, being fully detached from all earthly bondage. This is the consciousness in 4th dimension. In this state yogis are absolutely one with the god. This stage is revealed to only few great souls, as Sri Ramakrishna, Swami Vivekananda, Sri Ramana Maharshi, Swami Shivananda, Paramahansa Yogananda, Hildegard von Bingen and others. For most mystics Samadhi is the crown of spiritual life, but for Sri Ramakrishna it was the beginning of a new epoch of experience, as he explained.

The first four disciplines are external procedures to keep our body and character in a sustainable healthy condition. It is a preparation stage for Raja Yoga. They are needed in the progress of our spiritual path, whereby the third and fourth steps stipulate specially our physical body and the breathing function, the life stream. The last four disciplines are inner procedures to open our spiritual soul and mind for higher attunement with the absolute. The fourth discipline Pranayama builds the link between the said external and inner procedure. Dharana, Dhyana and Samadhi are the three progressive steps of meditation. Each of the three sub-Yoga arts of Raja Yoga, as mentioned before, appeals in their own individual way to manifest in us the philosophy of Raja Yoga, the realization of divinity in us through mastering our mind and spirit. To this Swami Vivekananda also says: "Believe nothing until you find out the truth yourself and that is what Raja Yoga teaches."

II-4 Hatha Yoga

Hatha Yoga has two forms of performances. The one form is the integration of Asanas and Pranayamas, the third and fourth disciplines of Astanga Yoga. Hatha Yoga provides a balanced condition of the body, mind and soul. Asanas keep our physical body in a healthy condition through several kinds of posturing practices. Pranayama keeps our astral nerves purified and increases the mental ability, about which we will know more in the later chapters.

The other form has a spiritual aspect. The word *hatha* consists of two syllables *"ha"* and *"tha"*. *"Ha"* means sun and sun being the source of active energy it symbolizes for positive life stream. This positive life stream is defined in Yoga as *Prana Energy*. About the philosophy of *Prana* we will know more in the next chapter. *Tha* means moon and so it symbolizes the passive energy, a negative life stream. Both positive and negative life streams are needed for the polarity on which the whole creation is based. Hatha is also interpreted as a forceful effort. Through the combined practice of Asanas and Pranayama, the basis of Hatha Yoga, our mind becomes concentrated in one center-point and thus the path of meditation is prepared towards the divine realization. The Hatha Yoga in its first form has become quite well known in the West through many Yoga Institutions. But in major cases, except in few well-guided institutes, it remains confined in a physical gymnastic form and at an intellectual level.

II-5 Kundalini Yoga

Kundalini is a divine cosmic energy. This spiritual potential is kept in a latent form symbolically represented by a sleeping snake in a coil at the lowest astral nerve center at the end of our spinal cord, called Muladhara Chakra. In the process of Kundalini practice, this latent energy called Kundalini Shakti is awakened in meditation with the help of Prana energy the basis of Pranayama and is raised step by step through the next five higher astral nerve centers upto the highest astral nerve center in our brain. This is a very distinct and most precious way to reach the state of absolute enlightenment. At the same time it is a very tough and difficult path, accompanied by psychic disabilities. There is no short cut in this path as many would like to have. Therefore, this long and entire path is to be followed only under a regular and intensive guidance of a very experienced and designated master and they are very rare. Kundalini practice has become quite popular in the West, but it is very much misguided, when used in many cases as substitute for drugs, causing severe psychic disturbances. Some more explanations on this subject we will find in chapter VI.

II-6 Mantra Yoga

Through constant repetition of mystical syllables in the form of sacred verses, praising all forms of divinity in form of singing or reciting during prayer meditation one becomes conscious of the deeper meaning of those texts and in the long run the prayers become a part of one's life and one perceives the divinity in self. The Mantra Yoga is also integrated in other forms of Yoga as in Bhakti Yoga. The texts of Mantra Yoga are in Sanskrit language. Therefore, the people born in other language circle as in the West may understand in some cases intellectually the meaning of those texts via translations but the texts will scarcely be able to touch their heart. The actual tonality of Sanskrit language cannot be given in Latin letters. So it would be advicable to use sacred verses or words of their own language or at least try as correct as possible for Sanskrit pronunciation. These forms of syllable repetitions are also found in other spiritual directions like Wazifas and dhikrs in Sufism or the prayer of the heart in Christian orthodox churches. It is a natural form of prayer for those, who feel inclination to pray.

Conclusion of Chapter II

On the whole to achieve the state of absolute knowledge of perception, following all the said Yoga paths are very difficult for us and it demands a life long immense discipline for inner engagements towards the path of divine liberation. So only a few blessed persons could reach such state of absolute knowledge also in India. Sri Ramakrishna, Swami Vivekananda, Swami Shivananda, Paramahansa Yogananda, Sri Ramana Maharshi were those blessed ones who reached the state of absolute union with the supreme Knowledge and divinely mastered the awakening of Kundalini Shakti. In chapter VII there are more explanations on Kundalini Shakti.

Anyone in the western world could achieve the goal of Yoga philosophy but the western life-style, especially at the present age and its environmental surroundings of high-tech expansions, like round the clock TV programme, excessive use of mobile phone, abuse of computer facilities play here a lot of hindrances for that purpose. Western life-style is directed extreme outwardly, whereby the philosophy of Yoga asks for more inwardly directed life, keeping a harmonious balance with the external life with its course of development.

"All Yoga methods as in India can not be directly overtaken in the West, because the life-style between East and West differs immensely from each other." This text was written by late Dr. G.S. Mukherjee* a well-known yogi in Calcutta, India in 1963, in his book 'Yoga and Our Medicine' (German edition, see Literature References).

After more than 37 years of the above text and more than 100 years of first introduction of Yoga in the West the differences in life culture between the East and West have increased enormously. Yet there are number of people in the West who are searching for inner life and are adopting methods of Yoga philosophy, besides others, so far as it suits their cultural field. Here the philosophy of Yoga builds the bridge between the two cultures.

In its natural state our mind is not quiet and concentrated but very fluctuating and absorbed in diverse thoughts, influenced by environmental causes like hectic modern high-tech life and injected by several kinds of mental pollution. As a result frustrations follow accompanied by psychic disabilities. To turn off this condition of mind and to bring our thoughts in concentrated form to get control over our nervous system we need to have a conscious control on our breathing, the Pranayama process, because mind and breath are spiritually united to each other as described by wise *Patanjali* in his Yoga-Aphorism. That the breath and mind act together can be observed when we get excited, our breath frequencies get faster and vice versa.

To the end of this chapter we may recall a text that Pranayama is essential on the path of Yoga to bring our mind at the center. Attaining the concentration of mind is a first step towards meditation. In this state of meditation we accumulate all spiritual power to achieve the higher knowledge. The spirit of Pranayama shall not exist only during practicing hours but that spirit shall be a constant accompanied and guiding part in every moment of our life like our breath.

---

* Dr. Mukherjee and the author were the co-disciples of the same Guru.

III

Prana—The Essence of Breath is the Fundamental Source of Pranayama

III-1 Definition of Pranayama

"Prana" is the first syllable of the combined word Pranayama, and "Ayama" is the second syllable. A very simple and literal interpretation of Prana means breath and Ayama means motion control, expansion of breath in space and time, as one can do in case of breathing cycles, because motion is associated with the ever cycling breath. Thus, Pranayama could be loosely translated as breathing control or just as normal physical breathing but that is not sufficient to explain its deeper sense. Then Prana is the vital life-energy, manifested from cosmic life, the breath of divine being and in our entire being there is a manifestation of Prana, the source of life. The Vedas, oldest scripture of Hinduism, celebrate Prana as godhead. So Pranayama deeply means the regulation or restraint of Prana energy in us. By learning the Prana regulation we learn also easily to have control over our own mind and we do not become the slave of the external activities of modern life. Therefore, there is a significant difference between the normal biological breathing and Pranayama. In the normal breathing process there is an autonomously continuing air exchange between our lungs and environment to meet the required physiological metabolic demands of the body to survive. The primal demand is the oxygen along with several other particles in the air. Thereby the cosmic manifestation of Prana, which exists in our biological breathing to build the link between the physical and astral body remains in unawareness.

III-2   Existence and Aspects of Prana

"India, China, Japan and to a lesser extent the Christian West have given birth to sages who realized their essential nature as a flow of intelligence. By preserving that flow and nurturing year after year, they overcame entropy from a deeper level of nature. In India, the flow of intelligence is called *Prana* (usually translated as "life force"), which can be increased and decreased at will, moved here and there, and manipulated to keep physical body orderly and young. As we will see, the ability to contact and use Prana is within all of us. A Yogi moves Prana using nothing more than attention, for at a deeper level, attention and Prana are the same—life awareness and awareness is life." These lines are quoted from the book "Ageless Body, Timeless mind" by Dr. Deepak Chopra. Prana is pervading in all forms of matter and yet it is not a matter. It is the energy which animates matter. The unused Prana (e.g. by death) returns to the great universal source from where it comes.

Through Pranayama performance our mind is then consciously brought to get hold of that subtle Prana, the omnipresent and infinite manifesting energy of universe, which is also the manifestation of spiritual breath, the breath of supreme being. Prana originates from self (Upanishad). It is the vital force, the cosmic life-stream existing invisibly in form of subtle vibration all over and in all beings, in all elements. To this Deepak Chopra writes: "Prana, the subtlest form of biological energy. Prana is present in every mental and physical event; it flows directly from spirit, our pure awareness, to bring intelligence and consciousness to every aspect of life. If you can experience Prana, you can begin to nurture and preserve it." This getting hold of Prana is done in co-ordination with our physical breathing and perceptions of our mind, because breath and mind are spiritually united (Patanjali). Hence, Pranayama is a spiritual way of breathing. Sri Yukteswar, the Guru of Swami Paramahansa Yogananda, said: "The cosmic consciousness is densely attached with the control of breath. The perception of mind initiates a process, that Prana energies flow correspondingly along with our physical breath and that is Pranayama." Thus through our imaginative power we can bring the Prana energy in every part of our body along with the breath.

"Other names of breath for life appear in Sufism, mystic Christianity and teachings of ancient Egypt. What is universally agreed on is that the more Prana you have, the more vital your mental and bodily processes" (Deepak Chopra). And Sufi Hazrat Inayat Khan writes; "....mysticism has been found on the science of breath. There is no mystic, whether Buddhist, Vedantist or Sufi, who makes use of another process than that of breath."

Normal breathing nurtures our physical body and Prana nurtures our astral body and the soul. Through our normal breathing we take up unconsciously more or less Prana, therefore, certain breathing techniques are developed and used so that more and concentrated Prana energy can be breathed in and that is then stored in our astral and causal body. "The various systems of Yoga in India teach many kinds of highly controlled breathing exercises, known as Pranayama, to balance the breath, but their actual goal is not to produce controlled and disciplined breathing under ordinary circumstances. Rather, paying attention to the breath is a vehicle for releasing stress and allowing the body to find its own balance. Once in balance, yogic breathing is spontaneous and refined, so that the refined emotions of love and devotion can be carried out through the body at all levels. When your cells experience the fullness of Prana, they are receiving the physical equivalent of these emotions", writes Deepak Chopra. He also writes, "Positive emotions, particularly love, increase Prana. Love is considered the most basic emotion that human awareness can feel; therefore, it is the closest to the source of life." The performance techniques of Pranayama are elaborately explained in the next two chapters.

During inhalation phase of Pranayama the neural signals of Prana energy in a form of mind's perception (emotion, vision) are carried up by afferent sensory fibers via spinal nerves to the brain (CNS). To Yogis the spinal nerve system is the passage to divine consciousness. During exhalation phase the efferent sensory fibers carry the Prana energy from the brain down to every part of our body. Thus, Prana stream in form of neural sensitive motor power is being spread all over our body and mind. Here, if needed, refer scientific explanation in chapter I-6 figure 5 for better understanding. The presence of Prana energy in us is subjected to constant radiation, vibrating out to the surroundings in form of our virtues, vitality and activities. So there is a constant need to regenerate Prana which is attained through regular Pranayama practices. Spiritually after exhalation Prana energy is recharged by the cosmic current and during inhalation we receive the regenerated Prana. To realize this we need a conscious perception capacity.

An important feature of Pranayama is the simultaneous practice of concentration, the prior stage of meditation, to bring our thoughts in one center point, a plane of consciousness. Therefore, during Pranayama performances it is adviced to direct the mind to our breath flowing in and out. There we gain knowledge to realize how the vital energy of Prana accumulates in us and thereby influences our body and mind to open the blissful path for our spiritual determination. Yet we have by nature limitation in our journey towards the higher realization, but through Pranayama and meditation we may once cross over this limitation The deeper inner relation between Pranayama and spiritual consciousness is revealed to us after a long period of sincere Pranayama practices with steady belief and inclination to spirituality. Yogis use this Prana energy very sensitively and consciously to awake the sleeping spiritual cosmic power potential in them (Kundalini practice). In our subconscious mind and in our nerve currents, see previous paragraph, there is an ever presence of Prana energy that creates a constant state of subtle spiritual vibration to keep our physical and psychic life as a living performance. This nature can be practically visualized in the following two paragraphs.

The respiration process is a self-active regulating system to modify our breath to the best of our demand when we are in sleep or when we are unaware of our breathing cycles, while we are awake (refer chapter I-6). Who then drives this self-activity without the presence of Prana? This presence of Prana generally we do not notice.

In November 1987, the author's heart had to be transplanted. After this a subtle and critical question came in his mind. Who of the both, the kind donator of heart or the author self is living, because the donated heart is still working whereas the original heart of the author is no longer living? The answer of this subtle question can be found only in the spiritual field. It is the Prana that unites the both—the donated heart and author—in one living unit. In this place a question may come up, how can this heart problem happen to me when I had so good physical and mental training. The first answer is the fate that no one can avoid. Second cause may be that I neglected my inner property totally at my advanced young age, being influenced by the exiting and stressed external Western life. On the other side, this gave me the chance to find my origin of life back for which I am most thankful.

Through regular Pranayama practices with much patience when we will be able to realize consciously that our breath is the breath of God, then we will become a living blessed soul. A living soul radiates physical and mental magnetism in its surroundings through invisible subtle vibrations because the waves of this magnetism are a manifestation of Prana energy. It is a long process and needs much patience and belief in Pranayama till the magnetism gradually manifest in us.

Our universe is immersed in a cosmic field, a field of fine divine resonance to carry out the knowledge of supreme intelligence to all directions. Prana is one of the aspect of this intelligence and so also resonates its energy constantly to all beings. Just a confident thought on Prana, "thought being the finest and highest action of Prana" (Vivekananda), our conscious mind will instantly plug into the resonance field of Prana to receive the blissful sensation in our breathing cycles. The depth of such experience depends upon the depth grade of conscious perception. The highest experience is attained when we can bring our mind in that higher state of revelation, which is Samadhi.

"For a person who really knows how to work with breath, there is then nothing he cannot accomplish; he cannot say of anything that it is impossible. Only it requires work; it is not only a matter of knowing the theory, but it requires the understanding of it. That is why adepts, the mystics, do not consider breathing only as a science or as an exercise; they consider it as the most sacred thing, as a sacred religion" (Hazrat Inayat Khan).

Both positive and negative aspects of life are an integrated part by nature in a human being. So it becomes a task to us that we learn to get hold of this negative aspects with the help of our breath. Mastering the breath through Pranayama means also mastering the self. In this place the author remembers an advice, what he received from his dear father at his age of 14 or 15. Father said, "At any time when you are in a state of negative tensions or of annoyance then you shall lower down your sight towards the earth and hold your breath (holding of breath intensifies the Prana energy) for a while and then mentally exchange your trouble with the neutralizing power of the earth." By that he might had meant the Prana-influence of the earth. With success I have practiced this when I needed.

Prana energy is also manifested behind the five basic elements of life: Earth, Water, Fire, Air and Ether. They provide us with Prana energies in different forms to sustain our life, which they have absorbed from *Akasha*. *Akasha* is omnipresent and so subtle in existence and all penetrating that it is beyond all ordinary perception. According to Hindu philosophy, *Akasha* is an infinite emptiness and it conceals all potentials of creation. It is a cosmic consciousness. First the impulse of Prana energy from the divine intelligence materializes those potentials in every form of universal existence and that we can perceive. Absence of these Prana elements will be the absence of life. "Nothing can remain alive when Prana is absent, because Prana is intelligence and consciousness, the two vital ingredients that animate physical matter" (Deepak Chopra). All living beings receive Prana energy mostly unconsciously through our senses like touching, smelling, tasting, drinking, eating, affection, inclination and so on. Every form we see, every thing that exists are evolved out of *Akasha* by the transcendental force of Prana. Gathering all these features in one concentrated focus we will realize that Prana, the infinite source of energy, is omnipresent behind our life. "The source of bodily desire is one, the breath. When the breath leaves the body all desires leave it also, and as the breath changes its elements—earth, water, fire, air and ether— predominate in the breath by turn, this being caused by the different grades of activity in the breath, so the desire changes" (Hazrat Inayat Khan).

The evolution forms the five subtle elements of *Akasha*, the earth, water, fire, air and ether. In this subject refer also the attributes of Prakriti-Shakti in chapter VI. The cosmic Prana mate-rializes those in an universe and that encloses all physical objects to become perceptible. Paramahansa Yogananda says, "When one percepts the god consciousness in own body, then one also reveals that the flesh is nothing else then the physical manifestation of the five elements earth, water, fire, air and ether". Through the follow-ing pictures, illustrated by figure 8 to 12, we will visualize in meditation how the nature provides us with the life holding Prana energies in different form of aspects.

Figure 8   The Earth.

Figure 9   Taking a bath in the holy lake Manashsharabar, Himalaya.

Figure 10 A fire celebration by a Brahmin priest.

Figure 11 The Air.
Symbolically pictured as the air is invisible.

Figure 12 The Ether.
Fragrance of rose is ethereal.

On Earth (Figure 8)

The mother earth sustains our lives providing us with grains, fruits, woodlands and a place for our physical bodies to live in fullness. The trees and plants growing in the earth receive rays of the sun and absorb carbon dioxide from the air and supply the needed oxygen. Thus, all what is stored by nature in the earth are energies, Prana, the nourishment of our bodies and souls. Thus, the earth in this or other forms provides us with Prana.

On Water (Figure 9)

Water is storing life sustaining energy. Without water there will be no existence of life. Water fertilizes the earth to grow grains and trees and so on which we need. It is soft and can be put in any form of pots or vessels and again it possesses a tremendous power. When we drink water we draw Prana in us. Taking a bath in the water we regenerate the Prana and we feel fresh. Amongst Hindus the bathing is a part of religious ceremony. Water in its pure form is full of Prana.

On Fire (Figure 10)

Fire provides energies in form of heat and light to keep us alive. The fundamental source of fire is the sun, the creator of cosmic energy. In Yoga, this cosmic energy is also defined as Prana energy what we receive in form of heat and light. To pay homage to this cosmic power the Hindus celebrate fire ceremonies and sun prayers at several occasions, such as during a marriage ceremony or during worshiping of deities. For Hindus fire has a purification aspect. The kindling of candles in a Christian Church has the same meaning.

On Air, Symbolically Pictured as Air is Invisible (Figure 11)

In each breathing cycles we exchange air to supply oxygen to our lungs. From the physical point of view this is a part of respiration physiology. According to the Yoga philosophy, the air is a spiritual aspect, the divine Prana energy of *Akasha,* which flows in us with each breath.

On Ether, also Symbolically Pictured (Figure 12)

Here to quote a profound text of great Vivekananda would be very appropriate. "Matter is represented by the ether, when the action of Prana is most stable, this very ether, in the finer state of vibration, will represent the mind and there it will be still one unbroken mass. If you can simply get to that subtle vibration you will see and feel the whole universe is composed of subtle vibrations." Ether is an expression of Prana.

The cause of this picture visualization (figure 8 to 12) is to become more conscious of the all pervading Prana energy of the nature and to refrain us from polluting our environment and by that damage the Prana, as it happens under commercial pressures in our modern high-tech age. Thereby we shall be also aware that nature itself is a creator and destroyer at the same time for eternal renewal process. Therefore, we shall be very cautious in our earthly performances to not to interfere unnecessarily (necessity is mostly an egoistic creation) in nature's process and thereby e.g. polluting the air, which injures the Prana energy that we breathe. Pranayama lifts up our consciousness to be alert to this subject.

The sense of Prana is omnipresent in Indian day to day life in several arts and forms. As for example, when a person dies, then we say Prana has left this person or a very deep relation between two persons is defined as bonded Prana or when a man feels very easy in his mind then he expresses that peace of Prana is manifested in him. "In India the body is perceived first as a product of consciousness and secondly as a material object. Conserving Prana is considered extremely important" (Deepak Chopra).

Even an unborn baby in mother's womb receives Prana energy, besides other substantial supplies for its growth, through mother's navel connection in the form of her caressing senses and through the subtle resonance of mother's breath movements and heartbeats. Thus, Prana becomes manifested in baby's whole being. But how many mothers are conscious of this invisible divine act, which makes their pregnancy happy and a blissful fulfillment period (except in case of natural or voluntary disorder appears in this period)?

III-3 Pranayama, the Healing Potentials

From the past passages we know that our entire being can be filled up with the vital energy of Prana by sincere practice of Pranayama and through meditative perception of Prana vibration. Specially our Solar-Plexus, a nerve center of Sensory Nervous System, a particular area between our navel and diaphragm accumulates Prana energy and that can be recharged repeatedly during Yoga-Breathing to compensate the energy consumption. To attain this state an intensified power of assimilation by the active presence of mind is very needed to follow our breathing cycles which is the active collector of Prana energy. Thus, through our mind and breath the Prana is brought to a higher state of vibration. This vibration can then be conveyed as healing potential to other living beings.

Whether we are conscious of it or not this state of Prana vibration generates within us also self-healing capacities to keep us in form and to protect us from any physical or psychic disorder at normal life. Yet in case of illness, when it happens to be, the inner healing energy supports the medical therapies applied to us. Behind this there must be also a lot of self-confidence and strong faith on this internal healing force of Prana current. These are not only theories, because the author himself experienced this realization during his time with heart trouble and is still experiencing through out the post operative time and that is keeping him in good condition.

Normally the Prana energy works in us in a state of balanced performance, neither too much nor too less. But due to some reasons, disharmony in life and so on, this balance may get disturbed. Then our body and mind fall into a certain negative states of sensitivity (less immunity for instance) and we are more inclined to disease. Regular Pranayama practice helps to take away the superfluous Prana or to supply more Prana to compensate the less and so the balance of Prana energy is fully maintained in us. Prana is the force underlying magnetic healing transformed in a mental healing. What we know as human magnetism is really Prana.

Through our breath and mind power we are also able to direct the healing capacity of Prana energy out of our solar-plexus to any part of our body. As for example, we unconsciously hold our breath for a while and feel a certain contraction near the solar-plexus area when getting a sudden stroke causing pain in any part of our body. Holding of breath intensifies the Prana energy and accumulates strength. Consciously we can also do the same, whereby we hold the inhaled breath for a while and convey the healing energy to the place of trouble in our body and exhale and repeat the process to get relief. Of course medical supports when needed are not be kept unattended in respective cases. Both together brings the success.

Thus, it is also possible to transmit one's own Prana energy to others when needed and even at a distance, to awake the dormant Prana energy for their own healing, so far as they are also willing to accept it and have faith on the subject. But this happens under virtuous conditions, whereby the healer, conveying the Prana, finds himself in a state of higher Prana vibration, a plane of super consciousness and does the healing service with an attitude of truthfulness, selflessness and out of boundless compassion. Such genuine healers are blessed but they are very few in number. The healers use up their Prana energy as much as according to the intensity of required healing force. Then they need to regenerate the delivered energies through Pranayama and meditation. Yet, even when we are not in that state of super consciousness, we shall not refrain from sending healing wishes to those who need the healing. Normally in our healing wishes there is also a presence of hidden Prana energy. Sending of health wishes is a very common practice and an old tradition everywhere and beyond any kind of boundaries without the knowledge of Prana as defined in Yoga and that helps too, so far it is full of compassion. "When the breath is developed and purified it is not necessary for the healer even to make an effort to throw his breath upon the patient, but the atmosphere that his breath creates, the very presence of the healer brings about a cure,

for the whole atmosphere becomes charged with magnetism"
(Hazrat Inayat Khan).

III-4 Different Forms of Prana

Prana is a collective definition of five individual Prana functions as
a wind (in Sanskrit Vayu) in the human body. They are: *Prana,
Apana, Samana, Udana* and *Vyana*, whereby Prana appears here as
a collective and also as an individual form. The difference between
Prana and Apana is that the Prana stream flows during inhalation
(afferent impulse) and the Apana flows during exhalation (efferent
impulse). Yoga Sastra reveals that Prana related to the heart and
Apana to anus are responsible for the variations in the growth
system of the body. The union of Prana and Apana is also Hatha.
Each of the above forms of Pranayama is also responsible for the
regulation of a particular autonomous physiological function of the
body, such as breathing, abdominal secretion, digestion, larynx-
pharynx activities and the venal-arterial system. To this Dr. Deepak
Chopra gives the following definitions: "Prana vayu regulates the
nervous system, Apana vayu regulates the excretion, Samana vayu
regulates digestion, Udana vayu regulates cognitive skills, speech
and memory and Vyana vayu regulates the circulation."

A detailed illustration of these forms of Prana may find very less
or even none access to the major readers of this book in our present
age. Particularly the correct pronunciation of the names, as they are
not commonly known in this western hemisphere, and the understanding of their functions will cause difficulties to them, even to a
wide portion of modern Indians. Moreover in the collective form of
Prana, these details are already enclosed. Considering this situation
these details of individual Prana forms are not further described
here.

III-5 The Value of Pranayama

Swami Sri Yukteswar, the Guru of Paramahansa Yogananda, says in
his book "The Holy Science" about the value of Pranayama. "We
have two forms of nerves, the voluntary one and the other involuntary one. We can put the voluntary nerves in action and can
control them, give them rest when we want, but not the involuntary
nerves. Yet we can get control over the involuntary nerves by the
performance of Pranayama to delay the natural decay of our
material body by giving rest to those organs who are controlled by

involuntary nerves. After such rest the involuntary nerves become fresh to work with new energy." And Swami Vivekananda explains in his book Raja-Yoga: "in a sense all the motion of the body becomes perfectly rhythmical through Pranayama performance and creates a gigantic battery of will. This tremendous will is exactly what is wanted to raise the power of spiritual knowledge. And that eliminates our spiritual ignorance. By that we are able to control our ego, so that it keeps the motor of life running but does not put its influence in our spiritual life." The conscious way of breathing brings a positive change in one's physical and psychic body, which steadily develops the personality. Through Pranayama we reveal astral purification in us. Physically Pranayama practices maintain the lungs elasticity longer than in normal life. Regular Pranayama practices manifest the Pranic power in us to enter into the deeper spiritual consciousness, to sustain our life with divine being and remove the veil of our ignorance. Pranayama practice removes the covering veils of Tamas and Rajas (see chapter V-3 and VI-5) in us and prepares our mind for inner meditation.

Conclusion of Chapter III

This chapter has brought us near to the vast and magnificent field of manifested Prana. Pranayama process revitalizes that Prana energy in us and to lead us towards the supreme state of consciousness and ultimately to reach the one Truth. True consciousness can not become unfolded without inner devotion. Consciousness in true self is the spiritual seed in us.

IV

Basic Preparations Prior to Pranayama Practices

Before beginning with Pranayama practices we need first to train ourselves correctly with some basic functions which are very common to all Pranayama variations—such as how to sit and how to breath. Adding to these two there are few other conditions which are also to be well observed prior to Pranayama performance, like mental foresight, physical conditions, place and time of practice, clothing, nutrition and at last certain necessary hints.

IV-1 Sitting Principles

Correct sitting posture is quite important so that Prana energy can flow unobstructed along with the normal breath stream into us and thereafter can spread out in all parts of our body. Normal blood circulation carries the oxygen (normal regular breath) all over the physical body. But the flow of Prana energy is a function of very subtle perception based on our nervous system, an ancient knowledge of Yoga Sastra. For the fulfillment of these aspects our spinal column takes up the principal function besides other parts of the body. Therefore, the spinal column must be brought knowingly in an upright position, while seated. Spiritually this form creates a top-bottom axis to connect the cosmos (*Akasha*) with the earth through our metaphysical body.

That is done when our back structure is kept in an absolutely vertical position to the ground in all four directions, resting the buttocks flat in one plane and thereby the shoulders shall be in a horizontal line. The head shall be kept slightly bent forward without tilting sidewise and the chin is pointing slightly towards the breast. The eyes are kept gently closed and the sight is lowered down and inwardly directed without pupillary movements. This will bring the mind gradually in a state of wanted quietness and concentration needed for Pranayama practices. The head in this position allows also an easy breath flow. In this head position attention shall be given that no tensions or pains come up in the neck area and the throat (Larynx) receives no pressure. The hands are kept relaxed on the lap having the fingers interlinked between the palms or the palms' backs are resting apart from each other on the respective knee according to the comfort of the practicing person. More about hand and finger formations, we will find in chapter V-2.1. Irrespective of sitting modes the upper part of the body shall be held always in the upright form in all variations of Pranayama performances. Then this has a two-fold effect. In one way the upright position of spinal column allows optimum space facilities for belly to inflate and breast cage to expand to the best function of the lungs. In another way it gives a free passage to the spinal cord for nerve currents to carry sensory signals of the Prana energy in a visionary form. In this process there shall be the presence of calmness in our body and mind without any haste so that mind can be tuned for perception.

Now to the sitting modes. The classical mode is the well known Lotus posture, see figure 13. But for most people in the western culture it will be either very hard or even not possible to perform this posture correctly, because their joints, specially all lower limbs below the waist are not flexible enough for the required formation. Besides that they are mostly not habituated for generations to sit on the floor. Except for those who are now well trained in yoga and meditation courses.

To meet the above mentioned problems there are alternative sitting modes. Hence, the figure 14 shows an easy sitting pattern, called Shukhasana for those, who can not do the lotus posture. So while sitting on the floor place your left foot under the right thigh and your right foot under the left thigh. If wanted the foots can be also placed in an opposite succession. This sitting posture is very commonly used.

To make Shukhasana posture more comfortable one can place a folded or rolled rug or a medium hard pillow under the buttock in a way that the upper body does not go out of balance, as shown in figure 15. This mode of sitting will cause for less stretch and tensionless thigh muscles and hip joints. In many Yoga classes now-a-days this method is very commonly used.

As a further sitting method one can use a so called meditation stool, which are very commonly used in the West for meditation purpose in yoga classes, see figure 16. But a care shall be taken that the stool ensures stability during Pranayama process.

Another possibility is to sit on an armless conventional chair, but not a sofa or alike. Correct sitting position on a chair is when there is a gap between the back and the back rest of the chair to get the spinal column support free. The height of the chair shall allow the feet to rest comfortably on the floor or use a foot stool or some other object in case of short legs. Legs shall be kept parallel to each other and vertical. Also one can use an ordinary stool instead of a chair as shown in figure 17.

Figure 13   Lotus posture

Figure 14   Shukhasana

Figure 15   Sitting on a rolled rug

Figure 16   Sitting on a meditation stool

Figure 17   Sitting on a chair

Figure 18 Sitting upright with vertical support.

In the above mentioned modes the seating position shall be on a comfortable but hard based plane. Persons with physical limitation using wheel chairs shall remain on their chairs and try to bring their spinal column in the aforesaid position so far as their physical abilities allow them to do so. Everyone shall have access to Pranayama in the given mode when one desires, so long no medical cause is against that. In extreme cases a person shall also be allowed to do Pranayama in Shavasana as shown in figure 24 in chapter V-2.4. We have two bodies, one is the physical and the other is the mental. For Pranayama the mental body is more essential to attune our consciousness towards the Prana energy flowing through us, even when the physical body is not by nature in desired form.

So that one can have the best performance on the physical aspects explained here, there is a need of training, especially the upright holding of spinal column, especially for those who have not yet joined in a yoga class. To start with the training for the back one can sit closely to a vertical wall or to a door panel and press the back vertically flat against the wall in its full length from buttock to shoulder, see figure 18. At the beginning one will feel some fatigue and eventual pain on the back within a short period during the holding of the said position. But with training and discipline one will overcome this state and gradually the back will be conditioned to sit upright for a longer period, at least 20 minutes or more, even without the support of wall. While sitting on the floor the knee-, ankle-joints are to be trained by often changing the positions and duration of posture and having a short relaxation in between, and slowly decreasing the intervals of altering the leg positions. Gradually in a time all joints will become flexible and habituated to sit longer in a posture.

IV-2 Breathing Principles

It will be very useful for this paragraph to review the Dynamics of breathing mechanism first in chapter I-5 and the figure 4. The three specific functions of respiration, the movements of the ribs, sternum and diaphragm are explained there. A simultaneous function of these three movements are the basis of Pranayama, which is yoga breathing. Most of all Pranayama variations are being accomplished through yoga breathing. But it is not possible to perform this simultaneous function at the beginning without practicing the individual steps first. Therefore, prior to Pranayama it is recommended to learn step by step how to bring the three involved functions in a simultaneous procedure during the breathe-in and breathe-out period.

First the sidewise expanding of ribs is to be trained during breathe-in cycles with the help of intercostal muscles by filling up the lungs volume to the utmost. The second training sequence will then be the forward and up movements of the sternum with the same respiration discipline. Then follows the training of diaphragm movements, inflating and deflating of belly during the respective respiration. When all these functions are individually well trained, then the next step will be the practice of bringing all three forms in one combined function.

The training is to be carried out always in one of the sitting modes as explained in the previous paragraph. Thereby care shall be taken that all relevant forms of posture remains unchanged and no cramp or tension comes up during training, it shall be done in a relaxed condition. Practices shall start with the exhalation first, following the rhythmic form of respiration cycle. While breathing in and out attention shall be given to the breath flow that it remains quite smooth and continuous without interruptions and force to bring uniformity in the respiratory duration. The change-over from exhalation to inhalation and vice versa shall be a smooth roll-over movement with a fraction of a pause what we unwarily do in normal breathing cycles.

In case of the breath-holding, a variation often used in Pranayama, the pause between inhalation and exhalation is voluntarily prolonged. But before doing such prolonged breath-holding one must have well practice in a regular form of only breathing-in and out. Otherwise a few longer breath-holding may become quite uncomfortable for many. First train the breath-hold function after the inhalation. When this function becomes quite easy then practice the breath-holding in reverse form between breathe-out and breathe-in cycle. If needed refer the part breath-holding in chapter I-3.

The following aspects are also to be considered while doing Pranayama practices. Pranayama shall be performed when the body and mind are not in an excited mood or in a hurry. In such cases take a rest for a while first, gently close the eyes and observe your present breathing rhythm and watch how the rhythm changes slowly from the higher rate of breathing sequences to a calming flow rate. While doing breathing listening to a soft music in a low volume also becomes very helpful for the mind to become calm. This is a concentration practice to calm down the nervous situation and bring back the presence of mind from the external world refocusing our attention into our inner life. Correctness of Pranayama breathing opens in us all relevant channels for Prana energy to flow in subtle forms for astral (ethereal) purification. And it is an engagement for our spiritual advancement.

IV-3 Mental Foresight and Preparation

Though Pranayama practices have to do with our breathing cycles, but they do not fall in the category of any kind of gymnastic training where breathing becomes a passive function, as already explained in chapter I-7. Pranayama is an active process to integrate consciously the yoga breathing and our thoughts in one controlled concept of divine perception. A further concept of such breathing is the receiving of Prana energy during each inhalation, while achieving the gradual banishment of egoism and ignorance during each exhalation and the realization of the depth of Prana energy during each breath-holding period. Exhalation conveys also the Prana energy in a form of directing healing energy while doing the healing service. In many Hindu, Christian and other religious communities the healing services are regularly done.

Toward the manifestation of these concepts in the process of Pranayama practices we stimulate in us a sensory divine vision of

Prana energy. This gives then the impulse to our afferent neurons to carry our vision via spinal nerves to the thalamus region of our brain (CNS). Here we shall know that afferent neurons carry only the signals of the stimulus as they are produced by our senses without differentiating the qualities (good or bad, creative or destructive) of our stimulants. So we must be very conscious about the depth and quality of our mental stimulation. Thereby we remember that our sympathetic nervous system (SNS) encourages us to increase our mental activity and to promote higher concentration capacity to have a deeper perception quality.

Going few lines back to the subject thalamus it is to be noted that besides thalamus there is an another co-region in our brain called hypothalamus. But the hypothalamus, being responsible for other functions in our brain, is not a relevant subject here. The thalamus brings the signals of our sensory vision (Prana energy) to the conscious level of our brain. The response of this consciousness is then brought down to our entire being by the efferent neurons. Therefore, the more we become conscious of our senses in this subject the more we realize how the very presence of Prana energy in our physical and psychic beings gradually lifts up our divine attainment from the lower to the higher intensity. To get few more informations one may review the chapter I-6 once again. Hence we can also realize that the science of physiology can not be kept apart from the conceptions of spirituality. Rather the science of physiology gives a supplementary support to the spiritual knowledge.

Following the above we can realize the essentiality of correct sitting posture in Pranayama, so that the neural systems can better communicate our vision to and from our brain. Our brain is the place of absolute and pure consciousness, the supreme knowledge. At the same time our mind shall get free from all external influences and create a state of inner calmness keeping the spirit awakened to respond to divine Prana. So our mind shall be essentially ready to observe consciously our breath flow. The mind in our normal life is in a restless state of activities and fails to concentrate inwardly. Therefore, it is needed to bring down the mind in a condition of stillness before performing Pranayama. This is done by performing the well known Shabasana for a while (see figure 24 in chapter V). Thereby we shall concentrate on hearing the sound of our normal breath cycles. To observe the breath sound is a very good practice to have a calming effect in our nervous systems.

Mental condition to conserve Prana energy needs balanced and refined breath, nonviolent behavior and a reverence for life, loving, positive emotions, free expression of emotion, says Deepak Chopra. At last we must be aware that it is not a matter of quick success, but it will take months and years of sincere and devotional engagement in Pranayama practice and try to avoid the influence of intellect during the practice to reach the goal of higher concept. Then only and with the divine grace we may have the absolute perception of subtle bliss of Prana in us. Without these concepts Pranayama will not lead us toward the divine attainment, for what we are searching for. As most individuals cannot attain the real Samadhi, so I have used the words divine attainment as the steps of development that shall bring to the state Samadhi.

IV-4 Physical Conditions

Pranayama practices can not be beneficial when our physical body (also mind) is not in a well condition. All negative aspects of life, like sicknesses in airways (Asthma, cough and cold, etc.), lack of self confidence and self-discipline, aggressiveness, in one way laziness and a sleepy or fatigued mood or physical restlessness due to over cumulating activities, excessive sexual engagements and above all habitual smoking, which considerably diminishes the lung capacities are the hindrances on the path of Pranayama. The causes behind all these factors may be unavoidable individual circumstances or the effect of the imposing medium (TV, magazines, etc.) publication or just lack of proper guidance or education. However, all these features are the opposite elements to disturb the harmonious and balanced function in our body and mind.

Therefore, we shall be able to get rid of all these negative factors or bring them under our constant self control to become detached from these influences and provide facilities to have a pure and fit conditions of our body and mind. We shall find communication with Satsanga (association with persons of truth and goodness) to have a supporting atmosphere around us, instead of spending hours in meaningless gossiping or having destructive thoughts and so on. The practice of Hatha Yoga is the best form to give our body the fitness, calmness and desired sustenance for Pranayama as well as pleasant relaxation. It opens our faculty to have deep insight into our life. It gives an elasticity in our joints and muscles and allows controlled regulation of blood circulation for an excellent physical as well as psychic condition. It never creates any turmoil in us. Actually Hatha Yoga and Pranayama belong together. There are several Hatha Yoga institutions, where one can learn and practice different Yoga Asanas. Asanas teach us to get control over all parts of our body and thereby create certain mind constellations. Hence, it is advicable to perform Asanas first and later Pranayama. And the last meal shall be taken at least 1 hour before commencing Pranayama. Also there is no objection to perform Pranayama for women in menstruation period or during pregnancy, except some form of Pranayama disciplines. It is well adviced in such a case to consult an experienced Pranayama teacher, because self-teaching from a book may lead to unwanted complications. It is also quite common that certain kinds of breathing control are taught by midwives or gynecologists to pregnant mothers, whereby Pranayama can also be well adjusted.

IV-5 Place and Time of Practice

In the land of origin, such as in India, Pranayama in combination with Hatha Yoga is performed mostly in out-door at the bank of a river or in an open compound of relevant hermitages, where there is little rain and the winter is not too hard. In variable weather conditions practices are done in a room or in a covered area. Practices are mostly carried out at dawn, the early morning hours by sunrise or by sunset to avoid heat periods of the day. Pranayama practices at dawn hours are commonly preferred in India, because the sunrise hours are being granted as auspicious and holy and the cosmic vibration in this period is very subtle to radiate Prana energy as the air is then fresh and pure.

But to apply this idea in the countries of cold western climate is not possible. There in winter the sun rises at a very late hours and in summer the sun rises at very early hours and that does not benefit most of the people to practice Pranayama at early morning hours. Moreover, western life in morning forces us mostly to jump up from the bed and rush to the place of work and the hours of stress are full in action. So willing persons should find a suitable time and place to practice Pranayama and yoga asanas. If once the suitable time and place are established, then that shall be held to as a routine. Once the body and mind are tuned to a time for Pranayama, then a natural rhythm sets up in our physical and mental constellations which cares for regular inner readiness for Prana power to draw in and that shall not be disturbed by irregularity in practice hours. A rhythmic life creates harmony in us and that is not to be neglected. If for certain situations—vacation, social engagements and so on—the regularity can not be held, then drop the practice for that day or that period of absence and continue the practice again at the routine hours, when those situations are over. So Pranayamas shall not be performed by force at any means.

In view of the practicing place some thoughts are to be considered. Always use the same place. The place of practice shall have a calm atmosphere. The place or room shall be well-ventilated with fresh air for at least 10 minutes prior to practice hours. If climate permits windows shall be kept open during the practicing hours. Create a meditative atmosphere in the room with candles and incenses. Incense may cause itching in throat so place it at a distance or remove it before starting practice. Meditative music can be used before or after the practice hours, because during the practice there shall be a perfect silence without any disturbing elements to support the concentration in breathing process. But if anyone is unable to face the complete silence, especially in the western hemisphere then there can also be some kind of meditative music but in a very low tone and without any percussion instrument. In any case, no exciting or churning up pop music shall be used for obvious reason. Actually Pranayama is also a prayer performance, therefore, there shall be a praying atmosphere around us while we do Pranayama.

IV-6 Clothing

The sport garments like elastic track suits or slack dresses which are commonly used in fitness studios or other sport events and in yoga classes, are also appropriate for Pranayama practices. Only there shall be no tight fitted dresses or trousers with belt or jeans, etc., no shoes. Further a personal experience of the author; during Pranayama course one can put a light and middle wide shawl over the shoulders to cover the body. This gives a certain feeling of inner coziness or a kind of individual virtual shelter to protect our mind from external attention, which again induces meditative moods.

IV-7 Nutrition

For the conservation of Prana energy proper nutrition (pure water, fresh food) is very important. Besides the principal mission of nutrition to keep us alive, we also receive the Prana energy through nourishment for constant revitalization of our physical and spiritual properties. In this place the descriptions of the five elements in chapter III-2 may be reviewed. Therefore, attention is to be given to the natural quality in the food which preserves Prana energy, as well as to the quantity of the nourishing elements and in their composition for preparing meals and drinks. Thereby we shall keep the fact in our mind that both quality and quantity together have corresponding effects on our health, temperament and character.

The quality of foods and drinks depends upon how pure and natural they are and how good is the proportional balance of the elements like, carbohydrate, fat, vitamin, protein, mineral salts in assembling a meal. Consciously and spiritually speaking there is an intelligent intention of supreme creation behind all natural nourishing elements. So the best way in selecting our nourishment is to find possibly natural non-manipulated foodstuffs that contain Prana energy.

Parallely a moderate quantity of a day's meal portions, solid and liquid, depends upon how correct we can measure the required balance between the energy input and output to and from the body due to physical exertion after considering the basic biological demand. It is useful to know here that in most cases the amount of hunger and thirst are artificially kept at a higher level through wrong feeding habits from childhood, appetite animation on sight of food and drinks, social and created personal habits, and so on. This habit should come under our psychic control so that a relative and moderate habit might develop in consuming our daily meals. Of course in certain occasions—social gatherings and events— where the meal consummation is higher than normal, one shall make an exception and enjoy the situation without repentance.

Several articles and essays are regularly published about modern diet methods in books or in many weekly and monthly magazines of fitness and fashion, and there is no end to that. So also it becomes quite confusing to differentiate the vast varieties of suggested nutritional philosophy and its compositions such as raw diet, bio-products, functional foods and designer foods and vitamin supplemented foods and drinks. How many of them are really good and effective and how many of them serve the commerce or fashion is a matter of individual acceptance. Whatever our choice, flood of publications have efficiently effected the wider knowledge on nutrition theory amongst the general population.

The answer to the question of what is preferable vis-à-vis vegetarian or non-vegetarian nutrition depends generally upon the circumstances of climate, personal requirements, social and religious traditions and of available geographical sources of major nutritional elements. The geographical sources, except in remote areas like high mountains in Tibet where only meat is available, is not such a problem due to the modern global business system and transport facilities. The availability and variety of food have become in one way very large and on the other side many products are lacking of biological and natural substances. Further a high trend of more and more vegetarians is observed in the West, though here meat products are one of the major components of nutrition.

Based on the information above one shall consciously select one's suitable nutrition form, vegetarian or non-vegetarian without neglecting the taste habit and the digestive factor. Nourishment is not only for good health but also to feel pleasure. In any way one shall not be fanatic in analyzing and selecting the nutritional formulas and neglect the pleasure on a meal. Pranayama theory suggests moderate, natural, palatable and when acceptable vegetarian nutrition, when considering the Prana philosophy. It is better to have variations in our nourishment than to have one-sided dieting, except when medical causes arise. It can also be noted that in course of an intensive and long Pranayama practice the nutrition habit may change towards pure vegetarian nourishment according to individual experience.

IV-8 Hints and Preventions

- At growing age lung volume decreases in accordance with the diminishing process of lung and chest wall recoil elasticity, refer chapter I-2. An old person can also begin with Pranayama practice which will delay the diminishing process, in as far as there is no sign of medical problems.
- As already mentioned in chapter I-4 the yoga breathing is normally carried out through nose only. In exception when certain Pranayama practices use mouth breathing.
- Before commencing with Pranayama check that there is no need of clearing the bladder and intestine.
- No Pranayama practice if there is any sign of physical and mental disturbances. Break down the practice in case of any

uneasy feeling in any part of the body, especially in the brain during practice hours and take rest for a while in Shavasana. Continue the practice on next day when the conditions are recovered.

- At the state of miserable and sorrowful mind or when the body feels absolutely fatigued, then one shall not practice Pranayama.
- Also Pranayama shall not be performed by hypertensioned persons e.g., high blood pressure.
- It is not recommended to do Pranayama practices outside in a chilly and snowing winter climate.
- Only restricted yoga breathing may be practiced by Asthma patients only after consulting the doctor.
- Pranayama is a discipline of inner engagement and shall not turn into a blind duty. Avoid overdoing the practice out of enthusiasm.
- Keep body and mind relaxed to perform Pranayama. To achieve this state of calmness concentrate and keep watch on your normal breath flow for a while.
- Performing Shavasana for some minutes before and after practice will give an easy get-in to, respectively get-out of Pranayama practice.
- Though Pranayama and Asanas belong together yet they are not practiced at the same time. Pranayama is a separate practice, after performing Asanas.
- Pranayama is not meant for a collective practice. Lessons on Pranayama can be given collectively as in cases of yoga seminars, whereas the individual practices are solely conducted. At a higher degree of Pranayama practices individual guidance by a teacher is needed.
- A beginner shall continue the practice for at least 10 minutes. Later the practice is extended for a minimum of 15 minutes or more when the individual ability that allows.
- Getting involved in external activities immediately after Pranayama diminishes its effect. Take a short period of silence and get gradually accustomed to normal life.
- During normal breathing within days cycle we also receive Prana energy, but we are not conscious of that.
- Well and long practiced Pranayama widens the ability of perception.

- The spiritual aspects of Pranayama let us feel good and continue an energetic life.
- Many say that Pranayama is not good and can harm our body and mind. It is true when it is practiced wrongly without proper guidance. It is the same virtue when one uses an instrument without knowing how to play it.

V

Variations of Pranayama and How they are Performed

V-1 Relation in Breathing Sequences to Inhalation-Breath Holding-Exhalation

At first one needs to know the importance of exhalation in Yoga-Breathing. Going back to the chapter I-2 (Vital Capacity) it becomes clear that in our daily life we do not use the full exhale volume (VC) of our lungs at each breath. Therefore, in yoga-breathing the exhaling duration is voluntarily stretched for two times longer than the inhaling duration for utmost utilization of the exhaling capacity. This gives a ratio of 1:2 for breathe-in and breathe-out. Simultaneously the expiration becomes active which is usually a passive function. Active expiration is widely used in life as in singing a steady tone for spiritual invocation. Stretched exhalation facilitates to bring more volume of air into the lungs through deeper voluntary inhalation, than the volume which is usually inhaled (increase of tidal volume). Thus, through voluntary stretching of respiratory duration in length and depth we learn to control consciously and efficiently our breathing performances and thoughts. This stretching allows the Prana energy to linger and spread over in our entire being. As the brain is vigilant in control of breathing so the concept of Pranayama ensures besides its spiritual aspects also utmost conditioning of our lungs and chest wall performances as well as optimum oxygen saturation in our body's blood circulatory system, specially in the brain. Through better blood circulation we look fresh and vital in appearance. At the same time, a vast field of spiritual energy is created behind by our sense of perception for Prana energy to act upon us.

Next to this comes the duration of breath-hold (refer also chapter I-3) in relation with inhalation. According to the Yoga culture the ratio for this is 1:4. That means the breath-hold period is four times longer than the length of inhalation. The final relation is then 1:4:2 for the breath sequences; inhalation-breath hold-exhalation. In certain cases breathholding after exhalation is also practiced, whereby the breathholding duration after exhalation is 1:1or even less in relation with inhalation, according to individual physical capacity, because after exhalation longer breathholding for 15 or more seconds can become quite uncomfortable. Thus, the final proportion of 1:4:2:1 for in-hold-out-hold stands as a standard ratio for all Pranayama practices, if not otherwise mentioned. Converting this ratio into seconds, the first step of lessons starts with 6 seconds for inhalation and so 12 seconds for exhalation without breath-hold period. Then increase the time relation gradually from 6:12 to 8:16 to 10:20 according to the development of regular practices and considering the maximum physical ability of your individual capacity. One can also start the training with the lowest time ratio 4:8, as in average the inhalation time is 4 seconds in a normal daily life. After reaching the longest possible time relation in the first lesson's step, then follow the second step of the lesson with the breath-holding period. This starts again from the beginning with time relation from 6:24:12 and gradually increase to 8:32:16 to 10:40:20 (40 seconds breathhold can be quite difficult for many. In that case reduce the hold period 25 to 50 percent to suit one's own ability). One can also begin from the lowest time ratio of 4:16:8. Here also the maximum personal ability for breathholding is to be considered. Effectively the gradual increase of time factors under the given basic ratios are part of the regular training of Pranayama, which are to follow, see position 4 of this chapter. Therefore, without proper training steps from the beginning it will not be easy to follow correctly the given time relations in breathing sequences, as we usually breathe in our habituated rhythm of breathing. So the best way to learn these relations in co-ordination with Pranayama variations is to have solid lessons under the personal guidance of a competent spiritual teacher, because the spiritual aspects are the basis of Pranayama. An experienced master knows how to advance the training steps physically and spiritually with the aspirants and also how to correct any false application during practices, such as voluntary overbreathing which can cause respiratory discomfort or improper breathing habits.

V-2 Additional Techniques used in Pranayama Practices

Prior to Pranayama practices we shall learn about the three kinds of techniques which are additionally used during Pranayama performances. They are Mudras, Bandhas and Kumbhaka, as called in Sanskrit language.

V-2.1 Mudras

Generally Mudra means forming. Mudras as a collective concept cover many operative aspects in Hatha Yoga and in Pranayama. Mudras are symbolical gestures or significant postures and actions of hands, fingers, eyes or other parts of the body to express inner and outer motivation and to achieve spiritual rituals. When Mudras are properly performed they gather cosmic energies closing a circuit of nerve currents in the body and lead us to gain consciousness for mystical experiences. One of the well known mudras is the bringing of both palms together during prayers as well as a greeting sign for Hindus. Out of the varieties of Mudras normally three types are used in Pranayama.

(A) Prana Mudra

Bringing the thumb, ring and small finger of the right hand together while the first and second finger remain loosely straight is called Prana Mudra (see figure 19 a and b). This form is used in Pranayama to control the breath flow individually through either of the two nostrils and to hold breath. To do that the thumb is placed on the right nostril and the last two fingers on the left nostril while the first two fingers are pointing towards the direction of third eye. By that the right or left nostril can be closed fully or partially while pressing

Figure 19 a Prana Mudra front view.   *Figure 19 b* Prana Mudra side view.

tightly or lightly the thumb or last two fingers on the respective nostril and so control the breath flow. If for any cause the right hand can not be used then the left hand can be used in an opposite form.

(B) Shanmukhi Mudra

Closing of ears, eyes and nostrils with the help of both hand fingers is called Shanmukhi Mudra, also known as Yoni Mudra as shown in figure 20 a and b. This technique is used to control the breath flow and simultaneously to switch off the outer senses like hearing and seeing. The correct way to do this mudra is when the thumbs close both ears and the first two fingers of both hands apply a light pressure on both eyelids and both ring fingers rest on nostrils flaps and thereby the last two fingers come to rest on the upper lip. The breath flow in the individual nostril is then controlled as needed with the help of pressure of the ring finger. In case of breathholding both ring fingers are used to close the nostrils. Thereby lift the elbows in a horizontal line. In the long run the practice of this mudra allows the wave of spiritual light and resonance of inner subtle spiritual vibration to arise.

Figure 20 a Shanmukhi Mudra front view.

Figure 20 b Shanmukhi Mudra side view.

(C) Usha Mudra

This is a classical gesture of palms commonly used during meditation. While seated the fingers of the both hands are interlinked and forming the palms as a bowl and gently placed upon the lap, as shown in figure 21 a. At this position one shall remain passive in mind to act only as a receptor for the divine stream before beginning and after Pranayama. Instead of Usha Mudra one can also perform Dhyana Mudra placing the right palm under the left palm, as shown in figure 21 b. In the following text only Usha Mudra will be mentioned. Then one can individually substitute Usha Mudra in

Dhyana Mudra during Pranayama practices, if it seems to be comfortable.

Figure 21 a Usha Mudra.

Figure 21 b Dhyana Mudra.

(D) Khechari Mudra

This is the mudra of tongue. Here the elongated tongue tip is rolled up back to touch the posterior palate while the lips are kept closed. This Mudra is performed in combination with Pranayamas to create better concentration to build a spiritual link in the vertical line with the fontanel, the place of higher consciousness.

V-2.2 Bandhas

Bandhas mean "lock". In advanced Pranayama practices relating organ functions are consciously locked to accumulate the Prana energy and to properly direct it's flow to a particular place for awakening the sleeping Kundalini. There are three kinds of bandhas; Jalandhara bandha, Mula bandha and Uddiyana bandha. Jalandhara Bandha in combination with Mula Bandhas unites Prana with Apana in our inner beings.

(A) Jalandhara Bandha

This can be interpreted as "chin press". In this technique while seated upright for Pranayama the head is lowered down slowly that the chin comes to rest closely on the breastbone without straining the neck muscle and thereby the larynx shall remain pressure free which means no glottal stop (see figure 22 a and b). It is not possible to hold the breath at deepest inhalation without a glottal stop. This manner of holding is unfavorable and could cause lung emphysema. Therefore, breath holding in combination with bandhas must be performed by a free larynx position but only with the help of the muscle power. The position of chin then produces a pressure in the neck's nerve area to obstruct the upward flow of Prana energy.

Figure 22 a Jalandhara bandha
front view.

Figure 22 b Jalandhara Bandha
side view.

(B) Mula Bandha

Mula Bandha verbally means root sealing but actually it is a contraction form of the anus. In Yoga culture the human perineum including anus is defined as Mula (root). The technique is performed when the muscles in the perineum areas including anus are so contracted as if they are pulled up towards the navel. Thereby the lower abdomen is squeezed in towards the backbone. These cause a sort of obstructing lock at anus area so that Apana, a sub form of Prana (see chapter III-4, different forms of Prana) can not flow downwards but rises upwards to unite with the Prana energy that is held by the chin press.

These two-locking methods are individually or simultaneously practiced in advanced Pranayama along with the act of breath-holding. This shows how much precious training is needed to perform such a complicated technique. So it is also obvious that this is not an easy subject of self-teaching but has to undergo the guidance of a master. At the beginning these two techniques are learned individually before practicing in combination.

(C) Uddiyana Bandha

It is a technique of holding the abdomen in a sucked up and in position for a while, see figure 23. This posture has a two-fold effect. In Pranayama process it pushes the Prana energy to flow upwards from the abdominal level through the spinal cord (afferent nerves) to the brain. From the physiological point of view it strengthens abdominal muscles and acts as therapy and prevention for digestive troubles, specially for constipation, as well as by stomach and intestinal weakness. This technique is performed in standing position with slightly bent knees while the upper body is stooped over so far that the palms are placed on the upper thighs to support the weight of the body. Then exhale deeply, hold the breath and suck up and in the upper part of the abdomen as much as possible and retain in this state for 6 seconds. The more the pressure of the palms is on the thighs, better is the drawing up of the abdomen. After the retainment stand erect and inhale deeply. Then take three deep respiration cycles and repeat the same technique. Repeat this sequence daily for 6 to 10 times and then rest in Shavasana position for a few minutes. This is practiced with an empty stomach (not immediate after a meal) and do not practice this technique if you have heart or stomach problems. Though these three-locking methods belong to the part of the Pranayama practices, but Uddiyana bandha is mostly practiced as an isolated exercise each time before or after doing Pranayama practices. Uddiyana bandha is also performed as a part of regular Yoga practices.

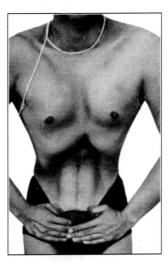

Figure 23   Uddiyana Bandha.

V-2.3 Kumbhaka

Kumbhaka simply means the breath-holding. In Pranayama besides the air we hold mentally the prana energy in us. The chapter I-3 has already reported on the subject physiology of breath-holding. Duration of breath-holding shall not be forced to go behind its breakpoint. With adequate training the breakpoint can be pushed in favor of longer duration yet it has a limit. In any case never penetrate the break point otherwise it will cause for problems like hallucination and so on as defined in chapter I-3. In Pranayama the breath-holding is an aspect of spiritual attunement. While performing Pranayama we tame our respiration cycle to hold breath for a given period. Simultaneous concentration on the breath flow holds us back from our intellectual concepts and our mind is then tuned to change over from outer to inner perception. By that we achieve the spiritual consciousness to make us free from earthly loads and begin to realize the presence of divinity in us. During the Pranayama process the breath-holding period, in combination with aforesaid "locks" (see Pos. 2.2 A and B), units the both Prana and Apana stream, the afferent and efferent impulses, in the spinal nerves and leads the combined energy to the Muladhara Chakra (see chapter VI-5) to wake up the Kundalini power. There are two forms of breath-holding:

(A) Breathe-in and hold. In Pranayama this is called as Antara Kumbhaka. In this state Prana unites with our inner consciousness and creates a field of willpower to raise us above all ill attributes of life.

(B) Breathe-out and hold. In Pranayama this is called as Bajhya Kumbhaka. In this state the hunger for Prana is created to become more conscious of Prana energy.

In the following the breathe-in and hold will be abbreviated as in-hold as well as the breathe-out and hold as out-hold. Before beginning the practice with in-hold function (the first sequence of breath-holding), a stability in deep inhalation and exhalation in equal length of timing is to be attained. Then at first hold the breath after a full inhalation for a few seconds only and exhale deeply. Take a pause for a period of 4 to 6 cycles of normal respiration after each breath-hold. Repeat this sequence for a few times. Then gradually increase the in-hold time up to 20 seconds or more, but avoid any overdoing. In case the hold duration causes a feeling of suffocation or any other discomfort, then the timing is to be adjusted to suit the personal ability. At arriving the stability in this function comes the training of adding the aforesaid "locks" during In-hold period, first the chin-press (Jalandhara bandha) alone for some time, then the anus contraction (Mula bandha) alone for some time and then both together. When the in-hold training becomes perfect then move over to train the out-hold function in same manner, but hold period shall be here no longer than 6 to 10 seconds. After achieving the training stability in both forms the breath-holding technique is added to some Pranayama performances. During all these practices keep the eyes softly closed and the body, specially the face in relaxed condition. Take the sitting posture as it has been individually selected from the given alternatives in the chapter IV-1 and hold the head in a position as it is also mentioned there. This is also practiced with empty stomach and no practices in case of slightest heart and chest cage problems.

V-2.4 Shavasana

Figure 24   Shavasana.

The figure 24 shows a posture for absolute relaxation. This figure is performed after each asana or a course of Pranayama during yoga practices. To perform this figure lay on your back keeping your head, neck and body in a straight line with the legs in a easy stretched form. Keep your heels in a close contact to each other, while the tows are sidewise open. Both the arms are kept stretched along the body with the upwardly open palms. All the muscular parts of the body must be in a well tension free condition. The whole body shall be so relaxed that one does not feel the existence of the body. Now lead your concentration along all the parts of the body to check that they all are really in a total relaxed condition, because a rest of tension in the body and mind may remain unattended. In this condition the respirations shall be quite normal. This posture shall be held for a period of at least 15 to 30 seconds. It needs a good practice to reach this state.

V-3 Bija Mantra

It is a form of spiritual recital during Pranayama courses to disclose our soul, the true self towards the divine being. Bija means seed or germ, enclosing in it the key sources of all beings, but alone this word does not give any sense here. Therefore, the correct form is Bija-Mantra. Mantra is a mystical hymn in syllable forms, the inspiring verses of *Veda* or *Upanishads*, recited or sung to praise the divinity and disclose our soul to its transcendental effect, see chapter II-6. The verses are of different length but the few short stanzas enclose the key meaning of the whole, as it is in case of seeds, are defined as Bija Mantras. In comparing with physics it is an atom.

In the school of yoga and spirituality in India, now a days some times also in the West in a more or less profound way, the dignified Guru gives an appropriate Bija Mantra to the initiated and sincere aspirant. During Pranayama courses this given Bija Mantra is then repeated continuously, silently or in low voice and in the rhythm of the breath by the aspirant as a form of inner devoted prayer. This Mantra repetition keeps our mind away from intellectual as well as scattered thoughts and transcends the mind by going deeply inside to attain a meditative condition and gradually feel the subtle vibration of divinity inspired by the meanings of Mantras. In the long run we can become a part of the divine Being so far as we have reached the state to abolish our egoistic self in the process of Pranayama life. Pranayama is performed in two ways, one is with Bija Manta and the other without. Pranayama practices with Bija Mantra brings the mind in the center point of our inner concentration.

The widest known Bija Mantra is the sacred syllable Om, the primal subtle sound vibration enclosing the key notes of all pervading existence. This subtle form of sound is not audible in the inner soul in normal life. This sound can be attained through deep meditation. In Om is the embodiment of the three mystical letters A, U and M. A represents *Brahma*, U *Vishnu* and M *Shiva* the divine trinity. Therefore, AUM or Om chanting is often done in most of all religious ceremonies or invocation amongst the Hindus. Patanjali says in his yoga sutra that God is the cosmic vibration of AUM. The three *Gunas* (attributes, qualities): *Sattva* the positive attributes, *Rajas* (passion character) the neutralizing force of cosmic matter and *Tamas* (darkness) the negative qualities are also confined in AUM. Through the mystical tone of Om when properly pronunciated and perfectly sung we invoke the omniscient guidance. The penetrating subtle vibration of the tone opens all channels in us for perception. We are then drawn to unfold the concealed divinity in our beings, the grade of enfoldment depends upon our spiritual advancement. Om is a sacred word, the symbol of Brahma the highest god of Hindus, which holds in self the quintessence of the Vedic philosophy.

At a certain advanced stage of experiencing Bija-Mantra, once upon a time the Mantra disappears and we become the Mantra. This is the hard path of Pranayama without the support of Bija Mantra. This can be explained with a story from *Chandogya Upanishad*. A Guru once asked a pupil to bring a fig and split it. After it was done guru asked what you see in it? The answer was a small seed. Then guru asked the pupil again to split the seed which was done. Again guru questioned what do you see in it? The answer was just nothing. Then guru said: out of this subtle "nothing" the universe is manifested. This is the truth, the absolute reality "*tat tvam asi*" that is you the higher being. Pranayama shall bring us to this point.

V-4 Pranayama Disciplines and Their Performances

Before doing any mode of the following Pranayamas be seated, as one has selected from the modes of sitting, for a while in a meditative mood using Usha Mudra to tune the mind and body for the success. During Pranayama performances keep your attention on the Prana energy in your breath stream. All breathholding modes are done using Prana Mudra. The enlisted Pranayama disciplines in this book are given in a certain advancing progresses. The advancing methods of teaching Pranayamas differs in the many schools of Yoga, so the given steps here may not coincide with one of them.

V-4.1 Basic Practice to Become Familiar with the Timing Ratios

Pranayama has two kinds of breathing duration, *equal phase* and *unequal phase,* but mostly the unequal phase is used in Pranayama. In the equal phase all breathing sequences inhalation, hold, exhalation are of equal duration. By the unequal phase the duration of breathing sequences differs from each other, see position 1 of this chapter. The following two courses are only for the beginners to train their feelings for the timing.

This has a timing ratio of 1:1:1:1 for in-hold-out-hold. Setting 6 seconds in this ratio initiate the training steps as given below. Sit erected and breathe through both nostrils

1st step	6:6	Only breathe-in and breathe-out for several times till the correct feeling for the timing becomes familiar to you.
2nd step	6:4:6	Breathe-in; hold and breathe-out in above manner till the hold function becomes familiar to you.
3rd step	6:6:6	Same as above with increased hold duration and get use to it.
4th step	6:6:6:4	Breathe-in; hold; breathe-out and hold. Out-holding is added.
5th step	6:6:6:6	In this practice the In-hold and Out-hold phases are in an equal duration, rest remains the same.

Reaching this 5th step repeat this daily for 5 to 15 rounds, as suits to you in 3-4 intervals and for a week long. Then increase the timing sequences in the above way to 8:8:8:8 ratio and repeat the cycles with 5 to 15 rounds daily in 3-4 intervals and that for a week long. Next change the time ratio in 10:10:10:10 and practice for a week again in the same way as before. Be conscious of the length of the duration in doing breathholding after exhalation that no uncomfortable feeling comes up. If uncomfort arises reduce the out-hold duration. During each interval relax in Shavasana, as shown in figure 24 or in a seated position. for about 30 seconds or more as one prefers.

Here the timing ratio is 1:4:2:1 for breathe-in; hold; breathe-out and hold. To initiate the training in this phase set also 6 seconds for inhalation in the beginning and follow the steps as given below. Sit erected and breathe through both nostrils.

1st step	6:12:6	Breathe-in; hold and breathe-out, train this till hold period becomes familiar to you.
2nd step	6:18:6	Same as above but hold period is increased.
3rd step	6:24:6	Same as above with further increase of hold period.
4th step	6:24:9	Same as above but out period is increased.
5th step	6:24:12	Same as above with further increase of out period. Train in this step well and then move to next.
6th step	6:24:12:3	In-hold-out-hold, till you are secure in out hold period.
7th step	6:24:12:6	In-hold-out-hold. Out-hold period is increased.

Reaching this 7th step repeat this daily for 5 to 15 rounds, as suits to you in 3-4 intervals and that for a week long without repeating the course-1. Then gradually increase the time ratio to 8:32:16:8 and then to 10:40:20:10 as done in course-1 with the same number of rounds, intervals and weeks, so far one is physically able to do so. Otherwise go so far as suits to you. During each interval relax in Shavasana or in a seated position as noted above. After these weeks of training it will give you a correct feeling in timing for the later Pranayama performance. It is to be noted here that timing in seconds is not an absolute figure that is to be observed with the help of a watch. Our attention shall be on our breath-flow and not on watch ticking. A person may count 6 which is actually a period of 5 seconds and for other the same counting may be in 7 seconds actual. Therefore, the main thing is to have a good feeling of time relation. Exhalation is double length of the inhalation, because each individual has their own rhythm of counting the second.

V-4.2 Ujjayi Pranayama

The word Ujjayi can be simply defined as conquest for power or success. As in this Pranayama the chest is lifted up and pushed forward which appears as a gesture of conqueror, so possibly for this reason the name Ujjayi has been given. This discipline consciously refers to our chest (thorax), thyroid gland and vocal chink (glottis) by the utmost expansion of the lungs. In this process a peculiar steady sound in an uniform pitch is produced owing to the partial closing of glottis during inhalation and exhalation. Also the characteristic of the yoga-breathing is to be observed while doing the following practices. Persons with thyroid gland problems or with high blood pressure should not perform Ujjayi Pranayama.

Course-1 Without Breath-hold and Bandhas

- Sit erected in a position according to your choice (review chapter IV-1) using Usha Mudra (see figure 21a).
- Stay for a while in this position with quiet breathing to become mentally and physically relaxed and observe your breath flow. Exhale well to follow the next.
- Lift up the chest and push forward and lower down the head, so that the chin can rest upon the chest near the collar bone. This is Jalandhara bandha (see figure 22 a and b).
- Keep the eyes softly closed without tension to have an inner sight. Keep also the mouth closed.
- Place your right thumb pad softly upon the right nostril to form the Prana Mudra (see figure 19 a and b) so that right nostril can be closed to not exhale through right nose. Thereby the small and ring finger shall not close the left nostril. Inhaling through both nostrils and exhaling through left nostril is a discipline of Ujjayi Pranayama.
- To begin with the yoga-breathing first exhale as usual. All Pranayama practices begin with exhalation.
- Then inhale slowly in an even and soft flow through both nostrils and fill up the lungs as much as one can without watching the time (mouth remains closed). Thereby keep your glottis squeezed to create a sound like *haa* tone. Then exhale in the same way only through the left nostril which then also creates a sound like *hii* tone. After the round take a short relax as said before and experience the vibration of sounds to realize how the Prana energy resonates in us. This is one round of Ujjayi.

After having a few rounds of this practice get relaxed for a while in Shavasana or in your seated position. Refer to the training charts in chapter VII for regular practice sequences.

Course-2: With Breath-hold and Bandhas

Here breathing sequences are same as in the course-1, except at the end of inhalation the breathholding (avoid overdoing) is done using Prana Mudra. And simultaneously Mula Bandha is used (See pos. V-2.2 B).

- Sit erected and exhale deeply and then inhale deeply through both nostrils while using Jalandhara Bandha.
- Hold breath as long as one can. Simultaneously use Mula Bandha, without releasing the Jalandhara bandha.
- After the breath hold period release Mula Bandha and exhale steadily only through left nostril with the sound as done above. During this period keep your mind attached to Prana energy. This is the end of one round.

After a few rounds, as suits to you, take a short relax as done before. Refer to the training charts in chapter VII for regular practice sequences. Physically this practice keeps the throat area, larynx, thyroid glands, glottis and the air ways in a healthy condition. Mentally it raises spiritual realization after long time of practice.

V-4.3 Alternating Breathing

This process is related to the following Viloma, Anuloma and Pratiloma Pranayama. In these disciplines as well as in the following other Pranayamas the breathing sequences will be performed in several forms of interrelated alterations to regulate consciously the breath stream, which is filled up with Prana energy for the physical and spiritual enrichment of our life. Physically these practices keep our airways clean and healthy and it improves the efficiencies of our lung functions and blood circulation. Thereby all physical organisms work in a rhythm and harmony and causing us to feel good and energetic. Mentally these practices eliminate tensions and nervousness by cheering up our attitude. Spiritually they are the purification process for *Nadis* the astral nerves, a principal purpose of Pranayama in the path of higher perception. Prana is the manifestation of the absolute being in the form of cosmic energy in us. Thus the body of Prana is our spiritual body. We need years of Pranayama practices to achieve perfection in Nadi purification. More about Nadi and Nadi purification we will find in a later paragraph.

Course-1: Left-in and Left-out / Right-in and Right-out Breathing

- Sit erected in your selected form for a while placing your palms on the lap in one of the aforesaid Mudras to quiet down your mind and to bring the attention to the breath. Perform Khechari Mudra as explained in chapter V-2.1 D and hold this position during the next steps.
- Exhale deeply at a steady flow through both nostrils.

- Use right thumb (Prana Mudra, figure 19 a and b) to keep the right nostril entrance closed till the following breathing sequences are over (no mouth breathing).
- Inhale deeply through left nostril (Left-in) for 6 seconds long.
- Exhale deeply through left nostril (Left-out) in a steady flow for 12 seconds long.
- Repeat this cycle Left-in / Left-out for 15 rounds or more or less according to personal ability without a pause in between.
- Then release the right nostril and breathe normally for a while thereby drawing your mind into contemplation on the spiritual purification energy of Prana.
- Now exhale deeply at a steady flow.
- Use right ring and small finger (Prana Mudra) to keep the left nostril closed till the next breathing sequences are over.
- Inhale and exhale through the right nostril (right-in / right-out) at a time ratio of 6:12 seconds in the same way as in the previous phase.
- Repeat this cycle also for 15 rounds as before.
- Then release the left nostril and breathe normally. This is the end of one round.

After having a few rounds, as suits to you, get relaxed for a while. Refer to the training charts in chapter VII for regular practices sequences. But do not hurry to reach a higher state.

Course-2: Left-in; Right-out; Right-in; Left-out Breathing

- Sit erected as done in the course-1 with Khechari Mudra and hold for the next steps and exhale utmost.
- Close the right nostril with the right thumb.
- Inhale deeply through left nostril (Left-in) for 6 seconds long.
- Change immediately the closing of the nostril from right to left using ring and the small finger of the right hand, Prana Mudra (figure 19 a and b).
- Exhale now deeply through the right nostril (Right-out) in a steady flow for 12 seconds long and immediately change over to inhale.
- Inhale deeply through the right nostril (Right-in) for 6 seconds long.
- Change the closing of nostril from left to right using right thumb.

- Exhale through the left nostril (Left-out) for 12 seconds long. This is the end of one round.

After having some rounds at the beginning get relaxed for a while and focus to your inner sight. Refer to the training charts in chapter-VII for regular practices sequences.

Course-3: Same as in Course-2 but with Breath-hold (Antara Kumbhaka)

- Be seated as you have done in the couse-2 and tune yourself to the inner life.
- Close the right nostril with right thumb as before.
- Inhale deeply through left nostril for 6 seconds as before.
- Close now both nostrils with right thumb and in combination of ring and small finger to hold the breath for 12 seconds. A state of Antara Kumbhaka with the help of Prana Mudra, see position 2.3 A of this chapter.
- Then keeping the left nostril closed release the right nostril and exhale deeply through the right nostril for 12 seconds at a steady flow.
- Immediately inhale deeply through the right nostril for 6 seconds long.
- Close again both nostrils as before and hold the breath for 12 seconds.
- Release then the left nostril keeping the right nostril closed and exhale deeply for 12 seconds as before. Take a short relax breathing normally then repeat the steps from the beginning.

Left-in / breath-hold / right-out / right-in / breath-hold / left-out builds one round of this course. Follow the increasing steps of time period, number of rounds, etc. in the chart of figure 25. At reaching the 9th step with the given time ratios in the said chart the last step can then be taken as a regular Pranayama practice. All the past practicing forms are then not repeated because this step integrates in it all the past practice forms in this discipline. Of course one may take one of the steps between 4th and 8th to one's personal limit. During this practice one will start to feel after a certain period the subtle vital force of Prana energy in the form of sweating, warm feelings, etc., showing that our astral nerves are getting purified having sensitive influence on our Chakra centers. The detail of figure 25 are also integrated in the training charts in chapter VII.

Timing for practicing the alternating Pranayama Breathing Course-3

Breathing Sequences	Step-1	Step-2	Step-3	Step-4	Step-5	Step-6	Step-7	Step-8	Step-9
				Given figures are in seconds					
Left-in	6	6	6	8	8	8	10	10	10
Breath-hold	12	18	24	24	28	32	32	36	40
Right-out	12	12	12	16	16	16	20	20	20
Right-in	6	6	6	8	8	8	10	10	10
Breath-hold	12	18	24	24	28	32	32	36	40
Left-out	12	12	12	16	16	16	20	20	20
Duration	0.5mo.	0.5mo.	1mo.	1mo.	2mo.	2mo.	2mo.	2mo.	Perm.

Figure 25

V-4.4 Viloma Pranayama, Intermittent Respirations

In this discipline there will be intermittent inhalation respective exhalation through both nostrils as well as either left or right nostril. Yoga-Breathing is to be observed as far as one is able to do so. How the intermittent respiration system shall work is explained as follows. Suppose during a steady and deep inhalation a person takes 8 seconds to fill the lungs with X ml volume of air. Then for the intermittent inhalation with same X ml volume of air the same person will use about 27 seconds. The intermittent exhalation functions in the same manner in the opposite way. The following figure 26 visualizes this fact with the help of a diagram for clearer understanding.

(A) Steady inhalation respective exhalation;
X ml volume of air in a time of 8 seconds.

= Respiration period without interval

(B) Intermitting inhalation respective exhalation;
Same X ml volume of air as by (A) in a time of approx. 27 seconds

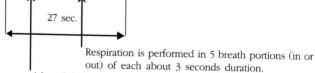

Respiration is performed in 5 breath portions (in or out) of each about 3 seconds duration.
4 breath-hold intervals of each about 3 seconds of duration.
During the period of breath-hold interval the exertion of breath mechanism (diaphragm, etc.) shall not be slacked to continue the next breathing (in or out).

Figure 26 Functional diagram of intermitting Pranayama.

In the following 6 steps in two courses the inhalation respective exhalation will be interrupted in different combinations as explained in the above figure 26. The duration of all interrupted inhalation and exhalation is more or less 27 seconds or as it suits to you. The non-interrupted inhalation is about 8 seconds and about 16 seconds for non-interrupted exhalation. Here all breathing forms, interrupted or not shall have maximum possible utilization of one's individual lung capacities. All following steps are performed in one's usual seated position keeping the mind attentive to the purpose of Pranayama. All steps shall begin after deep exhalation and the breath stream shall be in a steady flow through both nostrils with closed mouth.

Course-1: Interrupted Respiration with Breath-hold (in-hold)

Be seated as usual for a while and exhale deeply, then follow the steps below:

1st step   Inhale deeply with 4 interruptions for a time period of approx. 25-30 seconds, according to your ability and exhale deeply in a steady flow without break for about 16 seconds long. Repeat this step for 10 rounds.

2nd step   Inhale deeply without break in a time period of approx. 8 sec. and exhale utmost with 4 interruptions for a time period of approx. 25-30 sec. Repeat this step for 10 rounds.

3rd step   Inhale deeply with 4 interruptions in a time period as before hold breath for about 5-6 sec and exhale deeply with the same 4 interruptions. The timing for both breathing way would be about the same 25-30 sec. Repeat this step for 10 rounds.

Relax for a while as known after the rounds. Refer to the training charts in chapter VII for regular practice sequences.

Course-2: Same as in Course-1 but with Out-hold Breath and Bandhas

Be seated as usual for a while and exhale utmost, then follow the steps below:

1st step   Inhale deeply without break in a period of about 8 sec-hold breath for 6-8 seconds (In-hold) and exhale deeply in 4 interruptions—hold breath for 6-8 seconds (Out-hold) and then breathe normally. Repeat this step for 10 rounds.

2nd step   Inhale deeply in 4 interruptions—hold breath for about 16 seconds (In-hold) exhale deeply without break - hold breath for 5-6 seconds and then breathe normally. Repeat this step for 10 rounds.

3rd step   Inhale deeply with 4 interruptions, hold breath for 16 seconds in combination with anus contraction (Antara Kumbhaka plus Mula bandha (see pos. 2.3 A and 2.2 B of this chapter) then exhale with same number of interruptions as during inhalation, hold breath for 5-6 seconds and then relax in one or two normal breath. Repeat this step for 10 rounds.

After a few rounds take a short relax in a known way. Refer to the training charts in chapter VII for regular practice sequences.

V-4.5 Anuloma Pranayama

In this discipline of Pranayama the inhaling breath is drawn deeply in a steady flow through both free nostrils. The exhaling breath is to pass through a narrowed nostril created by the finger pressure of Prana Mudra. The slight pressure on the individual nostril shall create a soft resistance to get a gentle and constantly equal long flow either through both nostrils or through alternating left or right nostril.

The inhaling duration is being kept about 6 seconds and that of exhalation will then be about 12 seconds. This ratio 6:12 can be increased to 8:16 or 10:20 after a long and efficient practice of initial timing, as far as the personal ability allows. For that the guidance of a relevant experienced teacher would be needed. At a certain stage the process of in-hold respective out-hold of breath will be added with or without Mula-bandha (contracting of anus muscles), see position 2.2 B of this chapter.

Course-1: Only Inhale and Exhale

- After seated properly exhale deeply then inhale deeply through both free nostrils for ~ 6 sec long.
- Exhale deeply for ~ 12 sec long at an equal flow against the soft resistance of both narrowed nostrils, caused by the appropriate finger pressure of Prana Mudra.
- Inhale deeply through free nostrils for ~ 6 sec long.
- Exhale deeply for ~ 12 sec. long only through the left nostril against its soft resistance created by finger pressure of Prana

Mudra and thereby the right nostril is kept closed under the thumb's pressure.

- Inhale deeply for ~ 6 sec. long through both free nostrils.
- Exhale deeply for ~ 12 sec. long now only through the right nostril against its soft resistance created by slight thumb pressure and thereby the left nostril is kept closed with the help of small and ring finger. This is the end of one round.

After a few rounds, as suits to you, take a short relax. Refer to the training charts in chapter-VII for regular practice sequences. In the following courses the breathing characteristics will remain same as in this course, so they will not be repeated but only the breathing sequences will be just indicated with the indication exhale respective inhale.

Course-2: Inhale and Exhale with In-hold

- After seated properly exhale deeply then inhale deeply through both free nostrils for ~ 6 sec. long.
- Hold breath (In-hold) for ~ 12 sec. long.
- Exhale through both nostrils for ~ 12 sec. long against the soft resistance of narrowed nostrils.
- Inhale deeply through free nostrils for ~ 6 sec. long.
- Hold breath for ~ 12 sec. long.
- Exhale now only through the narrowed left nostril for ~ 12 sec. long, keeping the right nostril closed.
- Inhale through both free nostrils for ~ 6 sec. long.
- Hold breath for ~ 12 sec. long.
- Exhale now only through the right narrowed nostril for ~ 12 sec. long, keeping the left nose closed. This is the end of one round.

After a few rounds, as suits to you, get relaxed as in previous course. Refer to the training charts in chapter-VII to follow regular practicing sequences.

Course-3: Inhale and Exhale with Out-hold

- Sit erected and exhale deeply then inhale deeply through both free nostrils for ~ 6 sec. long.
- Exhale for ~ 12 sec. long against the resistance of both narrowed nostrils
- Hold breath (Out-hold) for ~ 5 to 6 sec. long or less, when needed.

- Inhale deeply for ~ 6 sec. long through both free nostrils.
- Exhale now only through the left narrowed nostril for ~ 12 sec. long, keeping the right nostril closed.
- Hold breath (out-hold) for ~ 5 to 6 sec. long or less, when needed.
- Inhale deeply through both free nostrils for ~ 6 sec. long.
- Exhale now only through the right narrowed nostril for ~ 12 sec. long, keeping the left nostril closed.
- Hold breath for ~ 5 to 6 sec. long or less and release. This is the end of one round.

In between all out-hold breath and inhalation take a short pause. After a few rounds relax for a while. Refer to the training charts in chapter VII for the practice sequences.

Course-4: With In-hold including Mula Bandha (anus muscle contraction) and Out-hold

- First exhale deeply then inhale deeply **through** both free nostrils for ~ 6 sec. long.
- Hold breath (in-hold) and simultaneously activate Mula bandha for ~ 12 sec. long.
- Release Mula bandha and exhale for ~ 12 sec. long against the resistance of both narrowed nostrils.
- Inhale free as above for ~ 6 sec. long.
- Hold breath with Mula bandha as before for ~ 12 sec. long.
- Exhale now only through the left narrowed nostril for ~ 12 sec. long, keeping the right nostril closed.
- Hold breath for ~ 5 to 6 sec. long.
- Inhale free as above for ~ 6 sec. long.
- Hold breath with Mula bandha as before for ~ 12 sec. long.
- Exhale now only through the right narrowed nostril for ~ 12 sec. long, keeping the left nostril closed.
- Hold breath for ~ 6 sec. long or less when feeling uneasy.

In between all out-hold breath and breathing-in take a pause with one or two normal respirations. After a few round of course relax for a while. Refer to the training charts in chapter VII for regular practice sequences. During the relaxed period (Shavasana) keep your mind concentrated to the power of breath nurturing your body and mind and making you more and more sensitive towards the Prana energy.

V-4.6 Pratiloma Pranayama

The respiratory sequences of Anuloma Pranayama, as listed above is just reversed in the respiratory sequences of Pratiloma Pranayama. Here the inhalation is against the resistance of narrowed nostrils, whereas the exhalation is through free nostrils. To simplify the following sequences the left and right nostril will be indicated as L or R or L+ R in case of both nostrils. The word "controlled-in" will mean to make the nostril passage narrow for respective L+R or L or R by using Prana Mudra, and also for breath holding.

Course-1: Only Inhale and Exhale

- Having seated erected exhale deeply in a normal flow.
- Controlled-in through L+R for ~ 12 sec. long.
- Exhale deeply through free L+R for ~ 6 sec. long.
- Controlled-in through R only for ~ 12 sec. long, keeping L closed.
- Exhale deeply through free L+R for ~ 6 sec. long.
- Controlled-in through L only for ~ 12 sec. long, keeping R closed.
- Exhale deeply through free L+R for ~ 6 sec. long. This is the end of one round.

After 4 to 5 rounds relax for a while as done before. Then move to next practice without repetition of this course keeping the breathing characteristics as before. Refer to the training charts in chapter-VII for regular practice sequences.

Course-2: Inhale and Exhale with In-hold.

- Having seated erected exhale deeply in a normal flow.
- Controlled-in through L+R for ~ 12 sec. long.
- Hold breath (In-hold) for ~ 12 sec. long.
- Exhale deeply through free L+R for ~ 6 sec. long.
- Controlled-in through R for ~ 12sec. long, keeping L closed.
- Hold breath for 12 ~ sec. long.
- Exhale deeply through free L+R for ~ 6 sec. long.
- Controlled-in through L for ~ 12 sec. long, keeping R closed.
- Hold breath for 12 ~ sec. long.
- Exhale deeply through free L+R for ~ 6 sec. long. This is the end of one round.

After 4 to 5 rounds relax for a while as done before. Then move to next practice without repetition of this course keeping the breathing characteristics as before. Refer to the training charts in chapter VII for regular practice sequences.

Course-3: Inhale and Exhale with Out-hold

- Having seated erected exhale deeply in a normal flow.
- Controlled-in through L+R for ~ 12 sec. long.
- Exhale deeply through free L+R for ~ 6 sec. long.
- Hold breath (out-hold) for ~ 5 to 6 sec. long.
- Controlled-in through R for ~ 12 sec. long, keeping L closed.
- Exhale deeply through free L+R for ~ 6 sec. long.
- Hold breath for ~ 6 sec. long.
- Controlled-in through L for ~ 12 sec. long, keeping R closed.
- Exhale deeply through free L+R for ~ 6 sec. long.
- Hold breath for ~ 5 to 6 sec. long. This is the end of one round.

Between each out-hold breath and breathing-in take a pause for one or two normal respirations. After 4 to 5 rounds relax for a while as done before. Then move to next practice without repetition of this course keeping the breathing characteristics as before. Refer to the training charts in chapter VII for regular practice sequences.

Course-4: With In-hold including Mula Bandha and Out-hold

Be seated erect and exhale deeply in a normal flow, then follow the next steps.

- Controlled-in through L+R for ~ 12 sec. long.
- Hold breath and use Mula bandha for ~ 12 sec. long.
- Exhale deeply through free L+R for ~ 6 sec. long.
- Hold breath (out-hold) for 5 to ~ 6 sec. long.
- Controlled-in through R for ~ 12 sec. long, keeping L closed.
- Hold breath and use Mula bandha for ~ 12 sec. long.
- Exhale deeply through free L+R for ~ 6 sec. long.
- Hold breath for ~ 5 to 6 sec. long.
- Controlled-in through L for ~ 12 sec. long, keeping R closed.
- Hold breath and use Mula bandha for ~ 12 sec. long.
- Exhale deeply through free L+R for ~ 6 sec. long.
- Hold breath for ~ 5 to 6 sec. long.

Between each out-hold breath and breathing-in take a pause for one or two normal respirations. Remember to keep your mind always conscious for the purpose of Pranayama. After 4 to 5 rounds relax for a while as done before. Then move to next practice without repetition of this course keeping the breathing characteristics as before. Refer to the training charts in chapter VII for regular practice sequences.

V-4.7 Kapalabhati Pranayama

This is a previous and moderate form of the next following Pranayama called Bhastrika. Kapalabhati Pranayama is practiced in one way as a preparation for Bhastrika and in the other way to keep the entire airways (see figure 3) clean for the general health and for other Pranayama performance. Even a small change of airway caliber effects the flow considerably and disturbs the free transmission of subtle flow of spiritual energy, the Prana. It has also a conditioning effect on our diaphragm. Therefore, it may be defined as the Pranayama of the diaphragm. Generally this practice also stimulates all abdominal organs and preserves the vitality. Even a few portions of Kapalabhati practice recharge our solar plexus with energy and quite soon one feels uplifted. The solar plexus is an important net of vegetative nerves and is very sensitive. Therefore, during the practice of Kapalabhati one shall induce his or her concentration on Prana towards the solar plexus to stimulate the afferent neural sensory fibers (refer chapter I-6, figure 5) towards Kundalini process. The Solar plexus is situated in a region in the middle of the breast between the costal arches and between the sternum and upper area of the navel, near the third spiritual energy center of Kundalini, called Manipura Chakra.

Performance Technique

As usual the performance begins with a few exhalations in a firmly seated or standing position to resist the following exhaling breath thrust. In this exercise the exhalation takes the main and active role whereas the inhalation acts as passive. The exhalations through both nostrils (mouth is kept closed) are forcefully thrusted out in a quick sequences through a very sudden contraction of abdominal muscles as well as pressing the diaphragm upwards. This way of exhalation will create a sound like a exhausting steam of a steam engine. The inhalations in between two exhaling thrusts occur in a natural and passive way while the abdominal contraction is released at the end of exhaling. Hence, the exhalation period is effectively shorter than that of inhalation.

One round of Kapalabhati consists of 10 to 15 exhaling thrusts at the beginning and one shall practice 4 to 5 such rounds per practicing period. Between each round do 2 to 3 normal respirations. The rounds and the number of thrusts are then gradually increased up to 8 to 10 rounds and the thrusts up to 100. Changes in higher numbers shall be practiced in the presence of a good experienced teacher to avoid any unwanted complications. All persons, men and women with different physiological disadvantages, like abnormal blood pressure lower or higher, uterus problem, nose bleeding, any kind of problem with retina, etc., shall keep themselves refrain from the practice of Kapalabhati. It is well recommended in this place to consult a physician about your physical condition in relation to this practice. Take a relaxed period as usual for a while after 1 or 2 rounds. Refer to the training charts in chapter VII for regular practice sequences.

V-4.8 Bhastrika Pranayama

Having a good practice in past Kapalabhati Pranayama it will be easier to conduct Bhastrika Pranayama. In Bhastrika, on the contrary to the Kapalabhati, both inhaling and exhaling breath thrusts follow alternately at a quick interval in an energizing force,which creates a sound like a blowing steam of a steam engine or blowing air of bellows of smith's shop from where the name Bhastrika (means bellow) comes. In Bhastrika as in case of Kapalabhati the exhaling breath determines the speed and rhythm of breath sequences.

The dynamic method of Bhastrika performance vitalizes the capacities of our physiological system, vascular, neural and the blood circulation due to the faster oxygen turnover. Hence, our brain is also energized for higher consciousness. So then the Prana energy is intensively activated in us. Due to this dynamic process one should avoid excessive practice in this discipline to avoid any unexpected harm to our breathing system. For the same reason all persons, men and women with different physiological disadvantages, like abnormal blood pressure lower or higher, uterus problem, nose bleeding, any kind of problem with retina, etc., shall refrain from the practice of Bhastrika. It is well recommended in this place to consult a physician about your physical condition in relation to this practice.

The opinion on Bhastrika practice relating to Kundalini process (see later chapter VI) a path to higher spiritual consciousness is viewed differently in the various texts of competent Yogis. For one the Kundalini process is in no way influenced by doing Bhastrika. Rather it would do harm to our physical and psychic body when practicing Bhastrika in anticipation of Kundalini success (B.K.S. Iyengar). For other Bhastrika is the best practice to purify the Nadis the astral nerves of Kundalini subject to bring a pulsation in

Kundalini energy to raise along the spinal cord (Swami Vishnu Devananda). However, with the presence of this difference the practicing technique does not differ as much as the opinion on the effect of Bhastrika practice. Therefore, one shall practice the Bhastrika Pranayama neither in anticipation of Kundalini experience nor fully neglecting its possibility but with humility and sincere open heart to receive a grant favor of higher consciousness if it ought to be. We shall remember that our strong beliefs can bring us to a higher goal.

Performance Technique

As usual be seated firmly and exhale deeply after a few normal breathing. This manner of beginning will be the standard function in the following variation of practices. Therefore, this instruction will not be repeated in the following.

Course-1

In this version there will be no interval between inhalation and exhalation while doing Bhastrika through both nostrils. So inhale in a quick and forceful motion and immediately exhale deeply in one speedy and powerful thrust by contracting the abdominal muscles and push the diaphragm upwards so that the exhalation becomes a dominating process. Thus, the inhalation and exhalation happen in a very quick sequences. This shall create a breathing sound in both way like a working steam engine and the resonance of the sound is being felt in the head region.

One round of Bhastrika Pranayama consists of about 10 such exhale thrusts in a quick sequences so far one can keep the proper speed, sound and pressure quality of the thrust. Otherwise one shall reduce the number of thrusts per round to suite to individual capacity. Initially there shall be about 4 rounds of Bhastrika per practice period. Then gradually increase the numbers of round up to 8 and the number of thrusts upto 25 at each round. But do not go beyond this limit to avoid exaggeration. It is known that continuity in small degrees brings better results instead of hyper activities. At the beginning about after 2 rounds, so far it becomes necessary, have a relax period as usual. Refer to the training charts in chapter VII for regular practice sequences.

Course-2

In this version the breathing process remains the same as in the first version except the use of alternating left and right nostril involving

Prana Mudra to close or open either of the two nostrils for Bhastrika practices. Do 2 rounds of Bhastrika each with about 10 exhale thrusts only through the left nostril keeping the right closed so as to build a function left-in / left-out. Then take a short pause in a normal respiration. Now change the nostril opening from left to right and do another 2 rounds of Bhastrika as before, keeping the left closed which then becomes a function of right-in / right-out. Having well practiced with these numbers of rounds in this discipline one can gradually increase the number of rounds and thrusts. Have a relaxed period as usual after 2 rounds at the beginning. Refer to the training charts in chapter VII for regular practice sequences.

Course-3

This third version differs from the second version only due to the addition of breathholding (Antarakumbhaka = In-hold) including chin press (Jalandhara bandha) and Mula bandha (Anus contraction). The hold exercises are carried out after each round of Bhastrika exhalation of 10 thrusts in the sequences as given below. Sit erected and exhale as usual.

- Do one round of left-in / left-out Bhastrika with 10 thrusts, as done in second version.
- Take a deep breath through yoga-breathing for ~ 6 to 8 sec. long.
- Hold breath (In-hold) for ~ 12 to 16 sec. long, so far one does not need to over stress the individual capacity. Simultaneously use Jalandhara and Mula Bandha to unite the Prana with Apana. Take a short interval in normal respiration with released Bandhas.
- Then do one round of right-in / right-out Bhastrika as before with 10 thrusts.
- Repeat the sequences of second and third step. This is the end of one round.

After having 2 to 3 rounds at the beginning get relaxed for a while as usual and observe your mind to go for inward realization. Refer to the training charts in chapter VII for regular practice sequences.

V-4.9 Shitsla Pranayama

The principal method of this Pranayama is the mouth inhalation through the tongue, brought out of the mouth and then rolled up to form like a straw pipe and enclosed around the lips. On the other side, the exhalation is as usual through both nostrils or alternately through left or right nostril. Just before the exhalation the tongue is then drawn back in the mouth to seal the lips for breathing out through the nostrils. There is a breath-hold period between breathing-in and breathing-out. This practice has a cooling and soothing effect to our organs specially in the summer months. It is not recommended to conduct this practice in presence of cold air or in the winter season. In India Shitala is practiced in hot periods. Shitali method is a sub-discipline of a main Pranayama features. Therefore, if there is an interest one may conduct this practice. In the following courses always begin with erected sitting and exhalation as usual.

Course-1

- Form the tongue around your lips as described above.
- Breathe-in deeply in Yoga-breathing through the pipe formed tongue with a hissing sound for about 6 to 8 sec. long.
- Draw back the tongue and seal the lips.
- Hold breath (In-hold) for about 12 to 16 sec. long or upto ~ 30 sec. so far you can suit that to your individual capacity.
- Breathe-out deeply through both nostrils for about 12 to 16 sec. long.

These five sequences build one round of Shitali in the first course. Repeat 15 to 20 rounds according to your choice. After each 5 rounds about get relaxed for a while as usual. As in all Pranayama here also the mind shall be attuned to the Prana energy flowing along the breath. Having well practiced in this step then follow the second course. Refer to the training charts in chapter VII for regular practice sequences.

Course-2

- Form the tongue as described in the first course.
- Breathe-in deeply as mentioned before.
- As before seal the lips after drawing back the tongue.
- Hold breath as in the first course.
- Breathe-out deeply only through the left nostril, keeping the right nostril closed.
- Repeat the first four steps as above.
- Breathe-out deeply now only through the right nostril, keeping the left nostril closed.

These ten steps, 5 with left-out and 5 with right-out, build one round of the second course. Repeat this round for 15 to 20 times at a time of your regular practice without repetition of the first course. In both first and second course the breath flow during exhalation can also be gently controlled using the technique of Anuloma Pranayama, see position V-4.5. Relax as usual at the end of the given repetition. Refer to the training charts in chapter VII for regular practice sequences.

V-4.10 Shitakari Pranayama

The method of this Pranayama mainly differs from that of Shitali in the formation of the tongue. Here the tongue tip is kept in touch with the upper palate in the mouth and then the lips are formed as in whistling while the mouth inhalation is performed. All the functions and practicing steps remains the same as in Shitali Pranayama and thereby let the tongue go to its natural position during exhalation.

V-4.11 Bhramari Pranayama

A buzzing sound like a bumble-bee is created in the throat (mouth remains sealed) during exhalation so the name Bhramari is given to this Pranayama, because Bhramari means bumble-bee. In this discipline the Shanmukhi Mudra is applied (refer Pos. 2.1.B of this chapter) to bring our mind to focus inwardly for inner realization.

Performance Process

- Be seated in your usual posture for Pranayama practice keeping the spine straight.
- Perform Shanmukhi Mudra as shown in figures 20 a and b.
- Inhale deeply in yoga-breathing through both nostrils for about 6 to 8 sec. long or up to 10 seconds long when well trained.
- Exhale deeply through both nostrils for about 12 to 16 sec. long creating a steady buzzing sound while the out flow is simultaneously controlled by the soft pressure of the ring fingers of both hands on the nostrils to get an even sound flow, as shown in Shanmukhi Mudra. One can extend the exhaling duration up to 20 seconds long according to the individual capacity. This is the end of one round.

During the practices you shall listen to the resonating sound in your inner being and as well as watch the possible light appearances in the eyes caused by the slight pressure of the first and middle fingers on the both eyes. At the same time switch off your external senses of hearing and seeing. This will bring you slowly in a state of meditation, a path towards mental and spiritual development. After doing few rounds as you can do get relaxed as usual. Refer to the training charts in chapter VII for regular practice sequences.

V-4.12 Murchha and Plavini Pranayama

These two Pranayama disciplines are no more in use though they belong to the Pranayama series. Murchha Pranayama is nearly the same as Ujjayi Pranayama but with very long breathholding period that may cause for many unwanted problems when not properly controlled. About Plavini Pranayama very little knowledge is available. Therefore, no further illustrations are given here.

V-4.13 Surya Bheda Pranayama

Passing through the previous forms of Pranayama we are now approaching towards the higher stage in Pranayama processes. This Pranayama form is one of them. According to the Yoga principle the breath air flowing through the right nostril appears as a warm stream whereas the breath stream through the left nostril appears as a cold stream. On the other side according to the Kundalini principle we have in our physical body three leading astral nerve channels (in total they are 72,000), called "Nadis" in the Sanskrit language. A detail illustration on this subject will follow in a later chapter, though many readers of this generation have more or less knowledge in the subject Kundalini. Two of these Nadis are called Pingala and Ida (see figure 27). The efferent and afferent nerve fibers of our Central Nerve System (CNS) are the Pingala and Ida of the Yogis (see figure 5). Pingala is associated with the right nostril and so it carries the warm breath stream whereas Ida is associated with the left nostril and carries the cold breath stream. Hence, the Pingala is also defined as a Solar Nadi whereas Ida as a Lunar Nadi. Thereafter the basic principle of this Pranayama is to inhale through the right nostril to have a warm flow, named also as solar breath and exhale through the left nostril which is then a cold flow and named as a lunar breath.

Due to this solar inhalation through right nostril the name of this Pranayama is given as Surya Bheda, because Surya-Bheda means the piercing sun rays. This name has affinity with the heat gain in the physical body while performing this Pranayama. Thereby the sweating of the body, an increase of the organs function indicates the emission of energy and that is an efferent function. In this stage our Sympathetic Nervous System (SNS) becomes active to adjust us physically and mentally to the Pranayama practices, refer chapter I-6 part SNS.

Effected by the concentration of mind the perceived Prana energy inhaled with the breath stream is then carried by Pingala the efferent current down the spinal column to strike strongly on the seat of Kundalini the last plexus of the spinal column. The Prana energy is then held there for a while by holding the breath to charge this Kundalini center and then the breath current takes the path of Ida Nadi and we exhale through the left nostril. This is a process of conscious breathing for higher attunement.

Conducting Sequences in Surya Bheda Pranayama

The following 5 points are the common repeating features, which are to be incorporated in all following courses of this Pranayama.

1. Sit in your usual posture keeping the spine straight and eyes gently closed.
2. Place your palms gently on your lap to form Usha Mudra (see figure 21a). Use Prana Mudra to control the breath flow and breath-holding. Perform also Khechari Mudra (see chapter V-2.1D) and hold that during the breath sequences of the courses.
3. Create a meditative mood and concentrate the mind to guide your thought on the seat of Kundalini. "The imagination can help you a great deal", said Swami Vivekananda.
4. First exhale fully to begin with the inhalation in the following courses. During inhalation and exhalation conduct yoga-breathing (see chapter I-5).
5. Instead of counting the time for the breathing duration it will be a spiritual act to repeat the word Om or any other sacred word. This sacred repetition stimulates Prana current to flow with our breath and creates in us a feeling of harmony and bliss. It would be good to review here the part Bija Mantra in chapter V-3.

Course-1: Right-in, Left-out Breathing

- Keep the left nostril closed using Prana Mudra and inhale at a steady flow for 8 to 10 seconds or as long as your ability allows through the right nostril against a soft resistance, created by the controlled pressure of your right thumb.
- Then close the right nostril and release slightly the finger pressure from the left nostril to create there a soft resistance during exhalation.
- Exhale deeply at a steady flow for a period of about 16 to 20 seconds or as long as you can extend the breath through the left nostril against the resistance. This is the end of one round.

Between each round do few normal breathing. A practice of 10 rounds per day in the beginning are being advised. Relax as usual after 2 or 3 rounds. Refer to the training charts in chapter VII for regular practice sequences.

Course-2: Right-in, In-hold and Bandhas, Left-out Breathing

- Close the left nostril and make the right nostril narrow to create a soft resistance during inhalation.
- Inhale at a steady flow for 8 to 10 seconds or as long as your ability allows through the right nostril against a soft resistance.
- At the end of inhalation hold the breath (In-hold) closing both nostrils and simultaneously use Jalandhara bandha (chin press) and Mula bandha (anus contraction) for about 30 seconds or as long as your ability allows.
- Now keeping the right nostril closed release slightly the left nostril to create a light resistance during exhalation.
- Exhale fully at a steady flow for a period of about 16 to 20 seconds or as long as your ability allows through the left narrowed nostril against its controlled resistance. This is the end of one round.

Between each round do few normal breathing. A practice of 10 rounds per day in the beginning are being adviced. Relax as usual after 2 or 3 rounds. Refer to the training charts in chapter VII for regular practice sequences.

Course-3: Right-in, In-hold and Bandhas, Left-out, Out-hold Breathing

- Close the left nostril and make the right nostril narrow to create a light resistance during inhalation.

- Inhale at a steady flow for 8 to 10 seconds or as long as your ability allows through the right nostril against its controlled resistance.
- At the end of inhalation hold the breath (in-hold) closing the both nostrils and simultaneously use Jalandhara bandha and Mula bandha for about 30 seconds or as long as your ability allows.
- Now keeping the right nostril closed release slightly the left nostril to create a light resistance during exhalation.
- Exhale at a steady flow for a period of about 16 to 20 seconds or as long as your ability allows through the left narrowed nostril against its controlled resistance.
- After exhalation again hold the breath (out-hold) by closing the both nostrils for 6 to 8 seconds or as long as you can extend the hold time. But do not go beyond the suffocation. This the end of one round.

Between each round do few normal breathing. A practice of 10 rounds per day in the beginning are being adviced. Relax as usual after 2 or 3 rounds. Refer to the training charts in chapter VII for regular practice sequences.

V-4.14 Chandra Bheda Pranayama

In Yogashudhamani Upanishad a Pranayama technique is written without given a name, which corresponds to Chandra Bheda Pranayama. In his book "Raja Yoga" in chapter V "The Control of Psychic Prana" Swami Vivekananda writes: "slowly fill the lungs with breath through the Ida, the left nostril, and at the same time concentrate the mind on the nerve current. Then hold the current there for some time...then slowly throw it out through the right nostril". This is just the sequence, which is exactly the opposite function of Surya Bheda Pranayama. Here the inhalation is through the left nostril, a lunar breath function and the exhalation is through the right nostril, instead of right-in and left-out as in Surya Bheda Pranayama. Therefore, the appropriate name Chandra Bheda is given to this Pranayama, because Chandra means moon the contrary of Surya the sun. So the Prana energy inhaled through the Ida Nadi, associated to the left nostril, creates an afferent current in us. It is also a function of the Parasympathetic Nervous System, the conservation of energy, refer chapter I-6 part PSNS.

In this section our mind perception lets the Prana energy carried by Ida, the afferent current, along the spinal column to strike strongly the center of the Kundalini seat. The Prana power is then held there for a while to charge this center with the help of breath. Thereafter the breath current takes the path of Pingala Nadi and we exhale through the right nostril. Chandra Bheda and Surya Bheda are the reciprocal Pranayama completion and thereby they create a balanced stimulation between the afferent and efferent nerve fibers, respective the astral Nadis Ida and Pingala. To not to over stimulate the Nadis and to preserve the balance Chandra Bheda and Surya Bheda Pranayama shall not be performed together on the same day but separately on alternate days. The breathing sequences of this Pranayama is the same as in Surya Bheda Pranayama except the reversal of the nostril function. To avoid any mistake the breathing sequences of Chandra Bheda Pranayama are listed in the following courses, which are similar to Surya Bheda but with reversed nostril function, as an independent version. The 5 common features written in Surya Bheda Pranayama are also to be incorporated in the following three courses.

Course-1: Left-in, Right-out Breathing

- Keep the right nostril closed and inhale fully at a steady flow for 8 to 10 seconds or as long as your ability allows through the left narrowed nostril against its controlled resistance.
- Then close the left nostril and release slightly the finger pressure from the right nostril to create there a resistance for exhalation.
- Exhale fully at a steady flow for a period of about 16 to 20 seconds or as long as your ability allows through the right narrowed nostril against its resistance. This is the end of one round.

Between each round do few normal breathing. A practice of 10 rounds per day in the beginning are being adviced. Relax as usual after 2 or 3 rounds. Refer to the training charts in chapter VII for regular practice sequences.

Course-2: Left-in, In-hold and Bandhas, Right-out Breathing

- Close the right nostril and make the left nostril narrow to create a soft resistance during inhalation.
- Inhale deeply at a steady flow for 8 to 10 seconds or as long

as your ability allows through the left nostril against its controlled resistance.

- At the end of inhalation hold the breath (In-hold) closing the both nostrils and simultaneously use Jalandhara bandha and Mula bandha for about 30 seconds, or as long as your ability allows.
- Now keeping the left nostril closed release the closed right nostril slightly to create a soft resistance for exhalation. Release also the both bandhas.
- Exhale deeply at a steady flow for a period of about 16 to 20 seconds or as long as your ability allows through the right narrowed nostril against its resistance. This is the end of one round.

Between each round do few normal breathings. A practice of 10 rounds per day in the beginning are being advised. Relax as usual after 2 or 3 rounds. Refer to the training charts in chapter VII for regular practice sequences.

Course-3: Left-in, In-hold and Bandhas, Right-out and Out-hold Breathing

- Close the right nostril and make the left nostril narrow to create a soft resistance during inhalation.
- Inhale deeply at a steady flow for 8 to 10 seconds or as long as your ability allows through the left nostril against its resistance.
- At the end of inhalation hold the breath (in-hold) closing the both nostrils and simultaneously use Jalandhara bandha and Mula bandha for about 30 seconds, or as long as your personal ability allows.
- Now keeping the left nostril closed release the closed right nostril slightly to create a soft resistance for exhalation. Release also the both bandhas.
- Exhale deeply at a steady flow for a period of about 16 to 20 seconds or as long as your ability allows through the right narrowed nostril against its resistance.
- After exhalation hold the breath (out-hold) again by closing the both nostrils for 6 to 8 seconds or so long as your ability allows. Avoid any suffocation. This is the end of one round.

Between each round do few normal breathing. A practice of 10 rounds per day in the beginning are being advised. Relax as usual after 2 or 3 rounds. Refer to the training charts in chapter VII for regular practice sequences.

V-4.15 Pranayama Processes for the Purification of Astral Nerves Towards the Spiritual Attunement

The principal purpose of Nadi purification through Pranayama practices is to preserve the smooth and non-polluted conductive sensitivities of our astral nerves for the perception of innermost knowledge. The pollution here means mental pollution out of our restless, scattered, egoistic, greedy mind world, as also previously mentioned. Purified nerves give peace in our mind and let the subtle vibrating current of Prana breath rise through the Shushumna the principal astral nerve canal in Kundalini. To reach the state of absolute result in Pranayama we need years of sincere practices. Following are two written methods of this purification.

(A) Swami Vishnu Devananda mentions in his book "Das grosse illustrierte Yoga Buch" (German version) about two ways of Nadi purification. The one is a spiritual path named as Samanu and the other named as *Nirmanu* which is a physical method, the Kriyas that are the same as Yama and Niyama of Astanga yoga (see chapter II-3). Samanu method shall only be practiced by advanced students of this field.

In Samanu Pranayama the duration periods of breathing-in, breath-hold and breathing-out are longer than in other Pranayama practices. They are about 16 seconds for inhalation, 64 seconds for breath-hold and 32 seconds for exhalation, including repetitions of a particular mantra syllable, Bija Mantra at each sequences and that asks for a good condition in previous Pranayama practices. These repetitions are conducted in a silent recitation at meditative mood. Simultaneously with the breath flow the concentration of mind is directed to the particular area of our physical body (Chakras) related to that Bija Mantra and one of the five elements. This needs to have a relevant sincere guidance from a profound teacher for the correct integration of these aspects. Therefore, this Pranayama is not included in the training chart.

Conducting Samanu Pranayama under the Guidance of a Teacher

- Be seated as usual and exhale deeply in a steady flow for the following breathing sequences. First step: left-in/hold/right-out, then second step: right-in/hold/left-out and the last step: left-in/hold/right-out.

- Closing the right nostril inhale through the left nostril so long till the16 repetitions of the syllable *Yam*, the Bija Mantra of air element, are inwardly recited. Then close the both nostrils to hold breath for 64 inward repetitions of the same syllable *Yam*. Then exhale very slowly through the right nostril for 32 inward repetitions of the syllable *Yam*. Take the help of Mala beads for counting the repetitions. During these period let your breath to be concentrated upon the Anahata Chakra (see figures 27 and 28) and on the air element that belongs to this Chakra.

- Close now the left nostril and inhale through the right nostril till the 16 repetitions of the syllable *ram* are inwardly recited. *Ram* is the Bija Mantra for fire element. Then close the both nostrils and hold breath for 64 inward repetitions of the same syllable *ram*. Then exhale very slowly through the left nostril for 32 inward repetitions of the syllable *ram*. Take the help of Mala beads for counting the repetitions. During these period let your breath to be concentrated upon the Manipura Chakra (see figures 27 and 28 in chapter VI) and on the fire element that belongs to this Chakra.

- Keep your sight fixed on the tip of your nose. Closing the right nostril inhale through the left nostril till the 16 repetitions of the syllable *tam*, the Bija-Mantra of the moon, are inwardly recited. Then hold breath for 64 inward repetitions of the same syllable *tam*. During the hold period imagine that the divine nectar is flowing from the moon through all Nadis of your body to purify them. Then exhale slowly through the right nostril for 32 inward repetitions of the syllable *lam*, the Bija Mantra of earth element. Here let your breath to be concentrated upon the Muladhara Chakra and on the earth element that belongs to this Chakra. Take the help of Mala beads for counting the repetitions.

(B) Parallel to the above Pranayama technique other forms of written Pranayama techniques, without specific name, are found in old sacred literatures like different *Samhitas*, the branches of *Vedas*. *Samhitas* means code of divine laws. There are techniques written, where several spiritual and physical process are precisely incorporated in one Pranayama pattern. They are classified as very subtle and contemplative disciplines to purify the Nadis. To perform such

Pranayama one needs a very accurate and sensitive guidance of a relevant master. Ancient Yogis realized that by Nadi purifying Pranayama the Prana energy flows in a balanced manner alternatively through the left and right nostrils, which creates a subtle stimulation in both parts of our brain, which in return brings harmony and peace in our life. It is a function of the afferent and efferent nerve current, the reciprocal counterpart of astral nerves Ida and Pingala. For the obvious cause no conducting process for such kind of Pranayamas are given here.

V-4.16 Pranayama on Basic Elements

According to the "Swara Yoga" text "Shiva Swarodaya", one of the branches of the vast field of Yoga, the presence of five basic elements can be percepted in our nostrils. It has been said there that each element has its own particular point of area in the inner nostril's surfaces which is allocated by nature. It is also said there that at each breathing sequence the Prana stream strikes only one of those five elements at their particular point at a time. But there is no constancy to this. So if the flow of Prana once strikes the point of earth element in the nostril, then in the subsequent breath it will strike an other element. This happens due to the physiological inconstancy of the air flow which changes time to time between laminar, turbulent or mixed air flow. This makes also difference in striking the subtle form of elements between the two nostrils. Suppose in a certain breathing phase the Prana strikes the point of water element in the right nostril, then simultaneously in the left nostril the fire element is struck, so is the yoga thesis here. Therefore, a very sensitive capacity is needed to feel the presence of individual elements in the nostrils when breath flow strikes that particular element. That is achieved only after long years of intensive training under a relevant teacher. For the obvious reason no further details are given here.

V-4.17 Nature Pranayama

After reviewing all past Pranayama patterns we come to a light pattern of Pranayama, that is presented here, a personal idea of the author. Let us go back to the chapter III-2 illustrating the Prana energy supply by the five elements. Whenever we are having a recreational walk or we make a rest in a natural area after a long drive then we can collect our thoughts to a concentrated point and feel the subtle radiation of Prana current emanating out of the elements. At the time of this perception we can begin to fill up our lungs with a deep breath to receive in us the Prana power.

So stand erect in a state of respect before nature with slightly bowed head and bring both hands in front of you and bring the palms together with the interlinked fingers to form the Usha Mudra. Then:

- Inhale deeply at a slow motion through both nostrils concentrating on the earth element.
- Hold the breath for as long as you can and try to feel inwardly what we receive from the earth in thankfulness.
- Exhale deeply at a steady and slow flow giving back your impurities. The earth element will dissolve those in self.

Repeat this cycle at any time at your choice in the same way with other elements one after the other knowing that each element has its own individual attribute and let these attributes enrich your soul.

Conclusion

If all these Pranayama practices are done on intellectual basis without spiritual attunement it will remain just as a sport exercise. The absolute being, the source of all supreme knowledge is so invisible and so infinite that we can approach this source only through symbols. After a long run with our inner devotion we may transcend the symbolic stage into the stage of higher perception to realize that supreme source in us, which is the transformation of duality in the non-duality. All these Pranayamas have such a symbolic character for opening the path towards the source.

VI

Kundalini—The Dormant Cosmic Energy in Human Being

The principal essence of Pranayama is the purification of Nadis, the sensory nerves in our astral body, charged by Prana current. In the terms of respiratory physiological science this can be interpreted as the function of afferent and efferent neural currents of our central nervous system, as written in chapter I-6. In spiritual terms through purified Nadis Prana current opens successively all subtle channels of our inner consciousness to attain ultimately the objectless perception of divine energy in our mind by prior awakening of the Kundalini, the dormant cosmic energy in us.

In the course of our daily life we face several hindrances to keep our mind stable on the path of inner consciousness. To overcome the hindrances the great Patanjali gave us steps of disciplines (see chapter II-3), like Pratyahara, Dharana and Dhyana following the highest step Samadhi. The integration of these disciplines in our life creates an invisible shield in us to protect our mind against the obstructing bondage influenced by external objects.

VI-1 Pratyahara (Withdraw)

This means conscious withdrawal of the senses from external objects to become free from the slavery of thoughts receiving in the mind. Then our soul finds its path towards the union with higher soul when our mind is free from the slavery of matter and we can master the external influences. This is the state of stable spiritual consciousness. But it is very hard to bring our mind in this state as the nature of the mind is constantly in a restless bubbling condition, a fertile field to be yoked by the distraction of material world. The best way to get over this condition is simply to watch the jumping mind without personal engagement in the happenings and wait and watch. At the beginning the mind will bring repeatedly enslaving thoughts to challenge us. Yet we will have to learn to ignore them. Thus, when the bubbling mind does not get any fuel of attention then the vagaries of mind will become less day by day until the mind surrenders under our control. This state of mind not allowing our senses to become self-active is defined as Pratyahara. "He who has succeeded in attaching or detaching his mind to or from the centers at will has succeeded in Pratyahara" wrote Swami Vivekananda in his book Raja Yoga. But this success does not come in a few days. It needs patience and a constant struggle with the self for years and years. In Pratyahara philosophy we learn to withdraw our senses from the distracting external objects and our mind becomes calm and liberated. In the next Dharana discipline we will learn how to guide our senses to become concentrated in a conceived purpose.

VI-2 Dharana (Conceived Concentration)

The theory of Dharana is to give a concentrated attention to a conceived (Dharana) thought on a particular object or subject by which one becomes deeply impressed. To achieve this state of our mind our attention shall be forced to focus exclusively on a certain point and realize this point as an absolute and nothing else. Such point can have many forms such as the tip of the nose or the point between the eye brows named as third eye, the place of divine vision or a small black point on a white board. Behind such a point lays a vast amount of metaphysical knowledge under the name "Bindu" in Hindu philosophy. One can use just a candle light keeping it at a certain distance from the eye sight. The chanting of the word Om in concentrated recitative repetitions in silence or any other sacred phrase that touches one's heart brings him or her in the state of higher sphere. In this way we can confine our consciousness to a limited thought without getting scattered to bring the steadiness in our mind, to mind, till this philosophy becomes an integrated part of our life. The next step is to deepen our consciousness and to gain inner knowledge involved in "Dhyana".

VI-3 Dhyana (Meditation)

This meditation is an inner process to bring our senses in a state where the conceived thoughts becomes totally absorbed in the inner concentration. In absorbed meditation we transcend our temptation, greediness and negative emotions. Recitation of mantras, the mystical tonal energy awakens the inner spiritual senses and leads to a tranquil meditation and the breath rate becomes calm and quiet. The vibrations of the mystical tone influence directly also the Chakras, the energy centers in our body, see figures 27 and 28. In this place it is to be mentioned that the meditation classes in many institutes are actually concentration classes. Meditation in a higher plane of mind's awareness goes beyond the space and time to free us from egocentric "I" in the illusionary field of Maya and we forget the existence of our physical presence. That leads us to the path of Samadhi, the super consciousness. In Hindu philosophy, the lotus flower is an ascetic expression of the meditation process. This flower grows in muddy water yet it remains detached and rises above the mud. The opening of petals represents the opening of inner knowledge. The shine of a blossomed lotus symbolizes the enlightenment in us when it comes from within. So also the energy centers 'Chakras' in Kundalini are represented by open petals of the lotus flowers.

Going through the aforesaid disciplines including Pranayama practices in our daily life we prepare our physical and mental sphere to direct the all penetrating Prana energy on the path of Kundalini invocation.

VI-4 The Evolution of Kundalini

The evolution period goes back in the early 500 A.D, the time when the Tantrism and Shaktism came up. A relation of Tantra philosophy is also to be found in the "Vedas" the oldest scripture (1500 B.C) of Indo-Arian philosophy. The Tantrism is a sacred act of secret rituals with mantra recitations and other ascetic practices to rise oneself into the transcendent sphere of the absolute spirit of Brahma the god of creation. So it will be not wrong to mention in this place that Tantra is never an indulgence act of sexual satisfaction as it is misleadingly practiced in some pseudo Tantra seminars and courses, especially in the west. One needs to open any esoteric magazine to find Tantra courses growing like mushrooms.

The Shaktism is a metaphysical tenet of power (Shakti) dedicated to the goddess responsible for the happening on the earth (nature's rule). Shakti is the manifested kinetic aspect of saguna Brahma while nirguna Brahma remains in the state of Samadhi as a source of all knowledge and spirit. Shakti is the female principle of cosmic energy and manifested in the earthly sphere as Prakriti. Prakriti literally means nature and refers to the basic matters out of which the world is moulded the primal nature. It is an active principle of saguna Brahma. Together she is the Prakriti-Shakti. She is the divine universal mother Kali or Durga. She is the wife of Shiva, one of the Trinitarian supreme spirits Brahma-Vishnu-Maheswar or Shiva. Through Prakriti's primal power (Adya-Shakti) Brahma is assigned to create, Vishnu to sustain and Shiva to destroy, the trinity aspect of God. The Prana evolution of Prakriti-Shakti in the universe is the manifestation of five elements; earth, water, fire, air and ether (space), refer to chapter III.

According to the Tantra philosophy there are three attributes of our senses; "eternal existence" (Sat), "eternal consciousness" (chit) and "eternal bliss" (ananda). In combination they express the Sanskrit word *Satchitananda,* the supreme bliss. "All creatures, from the highest to the lowest in the link of creation, are found eager to realize the *Satchitananda*", said Swami Sri Yukteswar, the Guru of Swami Yogananda. In Tantra *Satchitananda* is further defined as "Shiva-Shakti" the eternal union of Shiva the absolute being and Shakti the creative spirit of Shiva. Shiva-Shakti is the inseparable union of the reality and its creating power. In Tantra ideology the physical union of men and women is sublimated in the creative unity of Shiva and Shakti.

In the process of evolution the "Jiva" the innermost soul, the true self in the form of spiritual monad within us gets confined in the nature's tangle under the influence of Maya, the illusionary field of materialism and sensual lust. Jiva remains in this confinement till we learn to direct our true self back through our yogic life leading and untangle us from the claws of Maya and make Jiva free from its captivity. Tantra defines this process of entanglement as the awakening of Kundalini, symbolized in the rising of coiled up serpent. At the highest level of this process there is the revelation of *Satchitananda.*

The Prakriti-Shakti is manifested in our astral body as a sleeping Kundalini-Shakti, the coiled serpent power located at the bottom plexus of the spinal column. There the head of the snake is kept in a downwards direction, a concealment symbol of entangled Jiva. In the process of Kundalini practice the head of the snake is turned up which means Jiva-Shakti is on the path of freedom. Inclusive with Pranayama and Yoga practices the attributes of humility, faith and devotion are essential for the awakening process of Kundalini. The awakening of Kundalini-Shakti from her sleep is a deep psychological process and that asks for bright consciousness, balanced mind and meditation on conceived inner imagination as well as profound experience in Pranayama practice and technique to lift up the inborn hidden spiritual power in us. On the contrary, unprepared and unconscious awakening of Kundalini will do serious harm to us through the uncontrolled release of enormous psychic energy giving unbalanced impulses in the Chakra centers causing psychic crisis. More about psychic crisis see chapter VI-7.

VI-5 The Attributes of Kundalini Chakras and Nadis

According to the Tantra doctrine there are seven interrelated astral nerve centers (anat. plexuses) in our spinal trunk known as Chakras as depicted in the picture "Vitality level of spiritual consciousness," see figures 27 and 28. The Chakras are the subtle cosmic energy centers in our astral body in a gradual rise from the earthly element to the higher revelation of spiritual vitality. Along a hollow canal of this body known as Shushumna Nadi, which runs through the corresponding spinal cord of our physical body, the Chakras are allocated according to the level of consciousness vitality by the intelligent senses of Prakriti. The subtle meaning of chakras can be disclosed to us during and after sincere Pranayama practices and in an intensive silent meditation.

Muladhara (pelvicus plexus), the first Chakra is located at the lower end of Shushumna, the sacral plexus in the spinal column. Here rests Kundalini the coiled up snake in sleep, representing Prakriti-Shakti also named as "serpent power". The snake is also the symbol of healing and defines the protective aspects in many cultures, especially in Hindu mythology. For example one can find always in the picture of Shiva a snake around his neck. The next five ascending Chakras are Swadhisthana, Manipura (commonly known Solar plexus), Anahata (cardiac plexus), Vishuddha and Ajna (cavernous plexus) and they are located along the trunk of Shushumna (see figure 27). They represent the corresponding level of ascending cosmic consciousness. The seventh one is the Sahasrara Chakra the level of supreme-consciousness, located at the top of the Shushumna. In the physical plane this chakra corresponds with the Central Nervous System (CNS) in our brain, refer chapter I-6.

Further there are two other astral nerve currents known as Pingala and Ida Nadi, as already mentioned in chapter V-4.13. They run respectively right and left and are oriented along the Shushumna canal. Their upper end meets in the Ajna Chakra having Pingala on the right and Ida on the left side of the Shushumna, corresponding the right and left nostril. On the way down to their lower end at

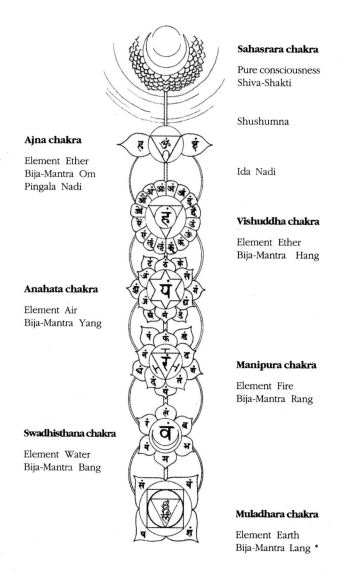

Sahasrara chakra

Pure consciousness
Shiva-Shakti

Shushumna

Ajna chakra

Element Ether
Bija-Mantra Om
Pingala Nadi

Ida Nadi

Vishuddha chakra

Element Ether
Bija-Mantra Hang

Anahata chakra

Element Air
Bija-Mantra Yang

Manipura chakra

Element Fire
Bija-Mantra Rang

Swadhisthana chakra

Element Water
Bija-Mantra Bang

Muladhara chakra

Element Earth
Bija-Mantra Lang *

Chakra centers front view
Figure 27   Vitality level of spiritual consciousness.

---

*   The exact pronunciation of Sanskrit Bija syllables can not be perfectly interpreted
     by Latin letters. Thus, several spelling forms are used in different publications.
     Therefore, the correct pronunciation should be learned directly from a teacher.

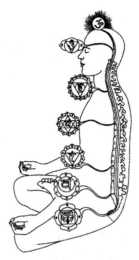

Figure 28   Side view Chakra centers.

Muladhara Chakra they move in a spiral way around the Shushumna canal. Thereby they cross all four middle Chakras at the center. At Muladhara Chakra they meet again on their respective right and left side of the Shushumna base. In the terms of respiratory physiology they are the main channels through which the afferent and efferent nerve currents travel (refer figure 5 in chapter I). The inhaling Prana current through the right and/or left nostrils flows down through these channels to strike the sleeping Kundalini. The exhaling Prana current through the right and/or left nostril rises up through the same corresponding channels. Therefore, these three main astral Nadis Shushumna, Pingala and Ida of the astral body are to be kept clear to transmit the Prana current by the purification effect of Pranayama practices.

The Chakras are individually characterized and symbolically represented by adequate number of petals of lotus flowers. The increasing number of petals from the first to fifth Chakra physically represents the respective number of nerves meets in a ganglion and spiritually they represent the growing dimensions of the sphere of consciousness and blissfulness. In the fifth plane at Vishuddha Chakra the consciousness of five elements is transcended in its pure form to Akasha, the ether. This the door way to absolute liberation. But only two petals stay in a relation with the Ajna Chakra and they symbolize the dual entity in us, God and self, the spiritual self and the earthly self. The solar and lunar nerve currents meets here with the God of knowledge in one unity. At this meeting point of the two petals is the location of the metaphysical third eye, the spiritual insight that sublimates the dualism to a non-dualism for Jiva to reveal higher spiritual consciousness. The concentration on this third eye is very common during meditation to focus and receive divine knowledge. The Sahasrara Chakra is symbolized by thousand (Sahasrara) petals. Here rests Purusha the personified spirit of Shiva in an union with his wife Durga, the Prakriti. It is the place where the highest unfoldment of Om the symbol of Brahma is realized. There are several other characteristic attributes of individual Chakras which are especially written in other relevant books on Kundalini. Out of them only two significant attributes are closely defined in the following paragraphs for this book of Pranayama.

One of the said two attributes is the combination of three basic aspects of our character which are to be positively generated in the physical plane for the qualitative development of the inner and external life. These are the "Will Power" (Iccha Shakti), "Handling Capacity" (Kriya Shakti) and the "Power of Knowledge" (Jnana Shakti). The united power of these three aspects is symbolized by the equal sided triangle and named as Tripurasundari, because they are also defined as the manifestation of three Gunas (review chapter V-3) of the universal mother the Prakriti Shakti Tripurasundari also symbolically unites the trinity power of God. Sattva Gunas the intelligent qualities of consciousness influence the area between 5th and 6th Chakra, Raja Gunas the energetic qualities influence the area between 3rd and 5th Chakra and Tama Gunas the material qualities influence the area between 1st and 3rd Chakra. Above the 6th Chakra there are no influences of Gunas.

The next significant attribute is the association of the five elements with five Chakras, because the universe as well as the physical and mental body of all individual living beings are formed out of the united energy of the five elements. So the Muladhara Chakra being the base is associated with the earth element whose aspect is the firmness or solidity. Following the Swadhisthana Chakra is associated with the water element whose aspect is the suppleness or pliancy. Next the Manipura Chakra the solar plexus is naturally associated with the fire element whose aspects are light and inspiration. Then the Anahata Chakra, where the subtle cosmic sound vibrates uninterrupted (Anahata), is associated with the air element whose aspect resonates our heart quality to carry the vibration of Prana energy. At last the purifying Vishuddha Chakra is associated with the fifth element ether, the spiritual aspect of purity. Vishuddha (purified) Chakra protects the Sahasrara Chakra (brain) from impure substances. From the sphere of Vishuddha Chakra matter is transcended in the spiritual sphere through the sphere of Ajna Chakra, the place of gaining eternal consciousness. In this sphere of Akasha the Ajna Chakra is the place from where the spiritual guidance radiates within us.

During Pranayama practices guiding the Prana energy to the individual Chakras in meditation we can incorporate all the afore-said aspects or qualities of Chakras in our life for spiritual experi-ences and advancement. The meditation on Ajna Chakra, on which the Yogis predominantly meditate, creates profound spiritual knowl-edge. Of course these results depend upon the intensity and sincerity of the meditation quality and not the quantity.

VI-6 Awakening of Kundalini

Under the spiritual guidance of an experienced teacher (Guru) one gains profound knowledge on the correct methods of practicing the Yoga Asanas, Meditations, Mantra recitation, Pranayamas as well as to sublimate the sensual desire of the body. By these practices Prana energy becomes highly charged. This energy is then brought down to the base of Kundalini through the Pingala and Ida Nadis, accompanied by the sensory power of mental projection on Kundalini to awake, which is transmitted by the efferent and afferent currents of our body's nervous system. Prana energy in the form of heat then causes for the uncoilment of the Kundalini Shakti to wake up from her sleep. Influenced by the Prana energy the awakened Shakti now rises upward through the Shushumna canal and crosses each Chakra one after the other on her way to the Sahasrara Chakra. And at each inspired Chakra the spiritual monad experiences a higher step of consciousness to reach step by step the state of absolute knowledge at last which is beyond time and space. "When the Kundalini is aroused, and enters the canal of the Shushumna all the perceptions are in the mental space. When it has reached that end of the canal which opens out into the brain, the objectless perception is in the knowledge space", wrote Swami Vivekananda in his book "Raja Yoga". By nature's law the upward journey of Kundalini Shakti is mostly interrupted at Manipura

Chakra and she comes down to her base. Through the intense and constant practice of Yoga processes Kundalini Shakti is repeatedly awakened from her slumber to continue her upward journey to reach at least the Ajna Chakra the cradle place of spiritual revelation. The journey from here to still higher Chakra point becomes then a spiritual hurdle. Coming at last at Sahasrara Chakra after long years of spiritual contemplation Shakti unites here with Shiva. This metaphysical union is defined as Shiva-Shakti or Purusha-Prakriti, in the physical field it is the union of human consciousness with the consciousness of the supreme divinity. This leads to the warm glowing vision of inner light as said by Swami Yogananda. At this moment *Satchitananda* is revealed to Jiva the innermost being and the true self becomes free form the bondage of matter. The real experience of this metaphoric state brings a spiritual change in attitudes and consciousness of one's physical and mental body forever. To reach this goal one shall be prepared for a life long related Yoga practices, yet at last the success remains at the mercy of God. The projection of this phenomenon in one's daily life will have a permanent spiritual influence on the consciousness by measured practices of Pranayama and meditation.

It is a phenomenon seldom attained when a mystical person succeeds in raising the Shakti to the heart center the Anahata Chakra. Only a very few great spiritual souls like Sri Ramakrishna and others, as already mentioned in chapter II, were able to raise Shakti up to the highest center Sahasrara Chakra and held her there for a relative longer period experiencing in trance the sparkling light of *Satchitananda*. Also a few spiritual souls of other religious cultures have had such spiritual experiences according to their relevant culture. They were and are the living examples of how enormous is the influence of Kundalini and alike experiences that bring higher spiritual consciousness to normal human life. Physical fitness and spiritual consciousness both together becomes an enormous gain in life quality.

In continuation of the aforesaid preparation for the classic form of Kundalini awakening process one needs to follow sincerely all the first seven of the eight disciplines of Astanga Yoga (chapter II-3). Pranayama, the 4th of those disciplines, is specifically explained in those previous chapters. By practicing the Pranayama one achieves the capacity to tune the mind to the astral and physical plane creating confident mental balance in one's life. To this mental balance once my Guru said to me "know that enjoyment without excitement is the sign of mental balance." This requires a deep relation between the pupil and the master. Therefore, in India traditionally we nurse a devoted relation with our Gurus who gradually initiate us on the correct process of training as well as transmits to us their magnetism so that we are able to recognize the inner Guru in our self. I remember what a blissful moment I had when I was brought to my late Guru at the age of 14 by my dear father.

Mental balance, also can be defined as emotional balance, creates a psychic control mechanism to neutralize the immense physical and psychic energy discharging out of the Kundalini awakening process. This balance gives the subtle and secure mental supports to transcend the arising energy waves in the body during the Kundalini awakening process as a wave of heavenly bliss. Practitioners can become frightened when they perform excessive Pranayamas or other Yoga practices out of their own enthusiastic obsession without genuine guidance of a master. They can face the outburst of typical crisis like heat rushing to head, heavy perspiration, constant trembling, emotional congestion, losing one's senses, convulsions, feelings of chaos, fear of death and so on. The fear of death escalates the crisis. Such a crisis can also appear suddenly in an unexpected situation as a spontaneous awakening of Kundalini. But the cause of such a crisis may not always be the Kundalini awakening. The question here is how often can such spontaneous awakening of Kundalini happen?.

VI-7 Kundalini Crisis and Conflicts

For a long time the Kundalini phenomenon was a subject of scepticism in the western world and even today. But based on modern scientific researches there are no more doubts on the presence of mystical high voltage energy behind the age old Kundalini awakening processes, initiated by ascetic persons practicing yoga in adoration, especially in India. This enormous psychic energy is kept by nature hidden in all human beings and conceals in itself a spiritual potential which after proper disclosing, as explained in the last paragraph, is able to lift up the quality level of sensory perception and physical efficiency to a higher state of clarity than the level of a standard form. At the end the state *Satchitananda* is revealed to one who unfolds that spiritual potentials.

The highest attainment of Yoga practices is to melt the consciousness of the ego self with the consciousness of the absolute.

Also the near death experiences are brought in co-relation with the quick Kundalini activities. I have experienced myself after a heavy heart infarct a state of near death. The experience brought in a flood of inspiring light and enormous blissful moment, yet I can not claim that the near death experience awakened Kundalini in me. Yet there is a relation between the near-death experience and Kundalini as in 70s indicated by Dr. Lee Sanella, director of the first Kundalini clinic in USA. Further the consumption of drugs or the energy transfer method from higher energetic human source, known in India as *Shaktipat* can become the cause of Kundalini power release. The reported negative symptoms of undesired physical disorders like suffocation, disturbed blood circulation, muscle cramps causing non-intended posture formation, burn out feelings, etc. are the effects of false motivated and fast food like practices that force the Kundalini to awake, especially when the life style and consciousness level do not coincide with the Yoga principle of life's mental and spiritual balance. Here the conflicts arise bringing the question; How many amongst the reported cases in the different countries of the world are the authentic form of Kundalini awakening ?

In ancient periods in India verified Yoga disciplines are practiced selflessly by the restricted number of specified Yogis on the path of awakening the Kundalini energy for spiritual realization of *Satchitananda* in a divine trance without notable crisis. They kept their experiences preserved from the wide public. Truthfully it is to be said here that in present India also there are fraudulent Yogis who perform occult practices in respect of Kundalini awakening. On the contrary to the restricted Kundalini practices as mentioned above, the opening of the Kundalini phenomenon to the west, e.g. biographies of Gopi Krishna and Swami Muktananda, has activated the Kundalini practices with wide popularity without having the distinctive background required for the purpose. To have a quick result when the Kundalini arousing process is forced by any means without prior conditioning then the Prana energy comes in the path of turbulence and rushes to the brain without halt at Chakra areas for gradual progression of consciousness. So without the proper guidance of an experienced teacher, when one is not well prepared and correctly motivated to practice Kundalini and to face the spiritual reaction on the energetic level of Chakra consciousness, then that will invariably cause the instability of mental and emotional balance creating psychic crisis or damage. Thus the cases of Kundalini crisis with their related symptoms pile up in the west. So that "Kundalini-Crisis-Clinics" in the 70s in USA were established (see previous paragraph) and later also in Germany "Psychosomatischer Fachklinik Heiligenfeld" was opened for the therapeutic care of affected Kundalini patients and to understand their churning up situation in spiritual crisis. Western psychologist tried at the beginning to explain this phenomenon as a special form of psychic disorder. The psychologist Vernon Neppe found in 1984 during the measuring of brain waves that in case of unusual activities of the temple lobes, like a certain form of epilepsy, which can be compared with the vision like Déjà vu experiences or light apparition. Since then several psychological studies were engaged to find the difference between the symptoms of Kundalini and psychic disturbance. (These texts were published in the German magazine Esotera, July, 1999).

Here are two quotes about the Kundalini crisis:

"Many people of western culture who awakened Kundalini without the required preparation, found themselves abruptly delivered to the turbulence of their transformation before their personality became enough steady to bare the energy explosion" writes Dr. Phil. Bonnie Greenwell, psychotherapist and lecturer of the Institute for Transpersonal Psychology in north California in her book Kundalini.

"Frequently the practices are functionally used without spiritual target in a western manner for different purposes and they are used in psychotherapy circles, in the sectors of sports and health or in self-realization groups" writes graduate Psychologist Liane Hofmann of Freiburg, Germany in a German magazine "Esotera."

Now the question may arise why the subject Kundalini is enclosed in this book of Pranayama. The answer is that the Pranayama practices have a strong link to the practices of Kundalini. Therefore, one who practices Pranayama shall know about the Kundalini, even when Kundalini is not necessarily being practiced.

VII

Training Charts for Pranayama Performances

Introduction to the Training Charts

In the following 10 training charts, Lesson 1 to Lesson 10 the Pranayama performances are programmed in a selected way that all important Pranayamas can be learned and practiced from the basic to the advanced stage in a gradual progress. Therefore, it is recommended to go through the lessons from 1 to 10 in the given weekly process, at least for those who are beginners in this field. The duration of each lesson's period is 12 weeks and thus, the entire program will be covered by 120 weeks. In the first 12 weeks only two forms of interchanging Pranayamas per day are to be performed, whereas in all the rest weekly lessons there will be three interchanging Pranayamas which are to be performed per day. One Pranayama-Week consists of 6 days. Keep one day in a week free for resting, to observe the effects of the practices on body, mind and spirit. In the same manner one Pranayama-Year consists of 4 lesson periods i.e. 48 weeks, so that the rest 4 weeks remain free to adjust rest periods. According to the numerology of Hindu philosophy the number 6 has an influence in the metaphysical counting system. Therefore, the training charts are also based on number 6.

The position numbers that are given in the first column of the 10 training charts coincide with the position numbers of the respective Pranayama positions in chapter V for easy review. The shaded fields in the weekly columns indicate the duration of the practice in weeks for the respective Pranayama. When a number appears in a shaded field that indicates the number of rounds to be performed per practicing period in that particular Pranayama. This is in the case of Surya Bheda and Chandra Bheda Pranayama (pos. 4.13 and 4.14).

As the weekly programs are not split in days so the number of rounds of these two Pranayamas shall be practiced in alternate days within the consecutive weeks. In general the number of performing rounds of the individual Pranayama pattern is given in the fourth column from the left.

The given program sequences and their duration periods may not suit everyone because of personal ability or of the stage of advanced experiences that one may encounter in Yoga schools. In this case the charts can be taken as a guideline to create personal charts. But such adjustment is to be preferably done under the guidance of a yoga teacher to avoid any unwanted mistake. In all cases we shall consider the slow growth as the golden rule in all aspects of our life to attain mastery particularly when following the yoga path.

Therefore, one shall be very cautious to follow the timing relation in respect of inhaling; breath-hold and exhaling as well as with the rounds of practices according to the personal physical ability and throttle the enthusiasm to go further.

At an advanced stage, say about a year of practice one can add Bija-Mantra, repeated silently in mind during the Pranayama performances while breathing-in and breathing-out, especially in the phase of breath-holding. The mantra Om or any other sacred prayer can be chosen as Bija-Mantra which would touch the inner being of the aspirants towards the higher perception. The Pranayamas like Shitali, Shitakari, Nature and Uddiyana bandha are not included in the training charts as they can be practiced at any time at one's liking, e.g. Shitali Pranayama is mostly done in the very hot days in the summer season. For Uddiyana bandha see position V-2.2 C.

The chart (figure 29) is for regular daily practices after the end of the training period of 120 weeks. The Pranayamas that are listed in this chart can be of any grade between the course-1 and course-3 and of any number of performance round selected out of the training charts. One can also add to or delete from the given number of Pranayama practices per day (3 per day in the chart) according to the personal inclination of the Pranayama practitioner. To have more than 3 Pranayama patterns per day it would be better to consult one's yoga teacher. In the long practice years it may happen that just one or two Pranayama patterns suit very much to one's life spiritually and physically and then that becomes for her or his very personal practice. Use the 4 empty columns of the chart for your personal choice of Pranayama under the advice of an experienced teacher.

Regular Pranayama performances per day after the 120 weeks of training.

Pos.	4.2	4.3	4.4	4.5	4.6	4.7	4.8	4.11	4.13	4.14				
Day	Ujjayi	Alternating	Viloma	Anuloma	Pratiloma	Kapalabhati	Bhastrika	Bhramari	Surya Bheda	Chandra Bheda				
1st.	***	***							***					
2nd.		***					***			***				
3rd.	***			***	***									
4th.		***					***		***					
5th.	***							***		***				
6th.			***	***	***									

Daily practice ends in Shavasana or in seated position for at least 2 minutes.

Figure 29   Daily Pranayama program after the end of 120 weeks training.

Lesson - 1   1st. 12 Weeks Program   2 Pranayama performances per day

Pos. No.	Pranayama Arts	Performance characters Timings, Thrusts, etc.	No. of Round	Training periods in weeks — 6 Days a week											
				1	2	3	4	5	6	7	8	9	10	11	12
4.2	Ujjayai Course - 1	no time limitation	6												
4.2	Ujjayai Course -1	no time limitation	8												
4.3	Alternating breathing Course - 1	a) 6:12 sec. unit	15												
		b) 8:16 sec. unit	20												
4.4	Viloma Course - 1 see figure 26	4 interrupts per breath	10												
4.5	Anuloma Course - 1	6:12—6:12—6:12 sec.	15												
4.6	Pratiloma Course - 1	12:6—12:6—12:6 sec.	15												

Figure 30   Relax in Shavasana or in seated position for about 15 to 30 seconds after performing each position.

Lesson - 2 | **2nd. 12 Weeks Program** | **3 Pranayama performances per day**

Pos. No.	Pranayama Arts	Performance characters Timings, Thrusts, etc.	No. of Rounds	Training periods in weeks 1	2	3	4	5	6	7	8	9	10	11	12 (6 Days a week)
4.2	Ujjayi Course-1	no tome limitation	10												
4.3	Alternating breathing Course - 2	a) 6:12 sec. Unit	15												
		b) 8:16 sec. Unit	18												
		c) 10:20 sec. Unit	20												
4.4	Viloma Course - 1 see figure 26	5 interrupts per breath	10												
4.5	Anuloma Course - 1	8:16 sec. Unit	15												
4.6	Pratiloma Course - 1	16:8 sec. Unit	15												
4.7	Kapalabhati	a. 15 exhale thrusts/round	5												
		b. 30 exhale thrusts/round	5												
		c. 40 exhale thrusts/round	5												

Figure 31 Relax in Shavasana or in seated position for about 15 to 30 seconds after performing each position.

Lesson - 3   3rd. 12 Weeks Program   3 Pranayama performances per day

Pos. No.	Pranayama Arts	Performance characters Timings, Thrusts, etc.	No. of Round	Training periods in weeks — 6 Days a week											
				1	2	3	4	5	6	7	8	9	10	11	12
4.3	Alternating breathing Course - 3 see figure 25	a) 6:12 sec. Unit	15												
		b) 6:18 sec. Unit	15												
		c) 6:24 sec. Unit	15												
4.4	Viloma Course - 2 see figure 26	4 interrupts per breath	10												
4.5	Anuloma Course - 1	10:20 sec. Unit	15												
4.6	Pratiloma Course - 1	20:10 sec. Unit	15												
4.7	Kapalabhati	a) 40 exhale thrusts/round	8												
		b) 50 exhale thrusts/round	8												
		c) 60 exhale thrusts/round	8												
		d) 60 exhale thrusts/round	10												
		e) 80 exhale thrusts/round	10												
		f) 100 exhale thrusts/round	10												

Figure 32   Relax in Shavasana or in seated position for about 15 to 30 seconds after performing each position.

Lesson - 4   4th. 12 Weeks Program   3 Pranayama performances per day

Pos. No.	Pranayama Arts	Performance characters Timings, Thrusts, etc.	No. of Round	Training periods in weeks 6 Days a week											
				1	2	3	4	5	6	7	8	9	10	11	12
4.2	Ujjayi Course - 2	as in lesson-2+bandhas	5												
4.3	Alternating breathing Course - 3 see figure 25	a) 8:24:16 sec. Unit	15												
		b) 8:28:16 sec. Unit	15												
4.4	Viloma Course - 2 see figure 26	4 interrupts per breath	10												
4.5	Anuloma Course - 2	6:12:6 sec. Unit	10												
4.6	Pratiloma Course - 2	12:12:6 sec. Unit	10												
4.8	Bhastrika Course - 1	10 thrusts both ways	4												
		15 Thrusts both ways	6												

Figure 33 Relax in Shavasana or in seated position for about 15 to 30 seconds after performing each position.

Lesson - 5　　　　　*5th. 12 Weeks Program*　　　　*3 Pranayama performances per day*

Pos. No.	Pranayama Arts	Performance characters Timings, Thrusts, etc.	No. of Round	Training periods in weeks　　　　　　　　　　　　6 Days a week											
				1	2	3	4	5	6	7	8	9	10	11	12
4.3	Alternating breathing Course - 3 see figure 25	a) 8:12:16 sec. Unit	15												
		b) 8:32:16 sec. Unit	15												
4.5	Anuloma Course - 2	a) 8:16:16 sec. Unit	10												
		b) 10:20:20 sec. Unit	10												
4.6	Pratiloma Course - 2	a) 16:16:8 sec. Unit	10												
		b) 20:20:10 sec. unit	10												
4.11	Bhramari	6:12 sec. Unit	10												
4.13	Surya Bheda	Course - 1	10												
4.14	Chandra Bheda	Course - 1	10												

Figure 34　　Relax in Shavasana or in seated position for about 15 to 30 seconds after performing each position.

Lesson - 6   6th. 12 Weeks Program   3 Pranayama performances per day

Training periods in weeks   6 Days a week

Pos. No.	Pranayama Arts	Performance characters Timings, Thrusts, etc.	No. of Round	1	2	3	4	5	6	7	8	9	10	11	12
4.3	Alteernating breathing Course - 3 see figure 25	a) 8:32:16 sec. unit	15												
		b) 10:32:20 sec. Unit	15												
4.5	Anuloma Course - 3	a) 6:12:6 sec. unit	15												
		b) 8:16:8 sec. unit	15												
4.6	Pratiloma Course - 3	a) 12:6:6 sec. unit	15												
		b) 16:8:8 sec. unit	15												
4.8	Bhastrika Course - 1	25 thrusts per round	8												
4.13	Surya Bheda	Course - 1	20												
4.14	Chandra Bheda	Course - 1	20												

Figure 35   Relax in Shavasana or in seated position for about 15 to 30 seconds after performing each position.

Lesson - 7

7th. 12 Weeks Program

3 Pranayama performances per day

Pos. No.	Pranayama Arts	Performance characters Timings, Thrusts, etc.	No. of Round	Training periods in weeks 6 Days a week												
				1	2	3	4	5	6	7	8	9	10	11	12
4.2	Ujjayi Course - 2	as in lesson 4	10												
4.3	Alternating breathing Course - 3 see figure 25	a) 10:32:20 sec. Unit	15												
		b) 10:36:20 sec. Unit	15												
4.4	Viloma Course - 2 see figure 26	4 iterrupts per breath	10												
4.5	Anuloma Course - 3	10:20:10 sec. Unit	15												
4.6	Prtiloma Course - 3	20:10:10 sec. Unit	15												
4.13	Surya Bheda	Course - 2	30												
4.14	Chandra Bheda	Course - 2	30												

Figure 36   Relax in Shavasana or in seated position for about 15 to 30 seconds after performing each position.

Lesson - 8   8th. 12 Weeks Program   3 Pranayama performances per day

Pos. No.	Pranayama Arts	Performance characters Timings, Thrusts, etc.	No. of Round	Training periods in weeks 6 Days a week
4.3	Alternating breathing Course - 3 see figure 25	a) 10:36:20 sec. Unit	15	
		b) 10:40:20 sec. Unit	15	
4.5	Anuloma Course - 4	a) 6:12:12:6 sec. unit	10	
		b) 8:16:16:8 sec. Unit	10	
4.6	Pratiloma Course - 4	a) 12:12:6:6 sec. Unit	10	
		b) 16:16:8:8 sec. Unit	10	
4.8	Bhastrika Course - 2	a) 10 thrusts	2	
		b) 15 thrusts	6	
		c) 25 thrusts	8	
	Bhastrika Course - 3	a) 10 thrusts	2	
4.11	Bhramari	a) 8:16 sec. Unit	10	
		b) 10:20 sec. Unit	15	

Figure 37   Relax in Shavasana or in seated position for about 15 to 30 seconds after performing each position.

Lesson - 9 — 9th. 12 Weeks Program — 3 Pranayama performances per day

Pos. No.	Pranayama Arts	Performance characters Timings, Thrusts, etc.	No. of Round	Training periods in weeks												6 Days a week
				1	2	3	4	5	6	7	8	9	10	11	12
4.2	Ujjayi Course - 2	no time limitation	15												
4.3	Alternating breathing Course - 3	10:40:20 sec. Unit	15												
4.4	Viloma Course - 2	5 interrupts per breath	10												
4.5	Anuloma Course - 4	10:20:20:10 sec. Unit	10												
4.6	Pratiloma Corse - 4	20:20:10:10 sec. Unit	10												
4.7	Kapalabhati Course-3	100 exhale thrusts	10												
4.8	Bhastrika Course - 3	a) 15 thrusts b) 25 thrusts	15 8												
4.13	Surya Bheda	Course - 3	10-30	10		10		20	20	20		30		30	
4.14	Chandra Bheda	Course - 3	10-30		10		10		20		20		30		30

Figure 38 Relax in Shavasana or in seated position for about 15 to 30 seconds after performing each position.

Lesson - 10 10th. 12 Weeks Program 3 Pranayama performances per day

Pos. No.	Pranayama Arts	Performance characters Timings, Thrusts, etc.	No. of Round	Training periods in weeks 6 Days a week											
				1	2	3	4	5	6	7	8	9	10	11	12
4.2	Ujjayi Course - 2	no time limitation	15	10											
4.3	Alternating breathing Course - 3 see figure 25	10:40:20 sec. Unit	15												
4.4	Viloma Course - 4	6 interrupts per breath	10												
4.5	Anuloma Course - 4	10:20:20 sec. Unit	10												
4.6	Pratiloma Corse - 4	20:20:10 sec. Unit	10												
4.7	Kapalabhati	100 thrusts	10												
4.8	Bhastrika Course - 3	25 thrusts	10												
4.13	Surya Bheda	Course - 3	10-30			10		20		20		30		30	
4.14	Chandra Bheda	Course - 3	10-30		10		10		20		20		30		30

Figure 39 Relax in Shavasana or in seated position for about 15 to 30 seconds after performing each position.

Conclusion

Breath is the gift of God and it is an ever present companion of us till we return to our origin, from where we came to experience life on earth. So we shall remain always conscious in thankfulness to this breath charged by Prana the cosmic energy.

"There is no mystical cult in which breath is not given the greatest importance in spiritual progress. Once man has touched the depths of his own being by the help of the breath then it becomes easy for him to become at one with all that exists on earth and heaven". (Hazrat Inayat Khan)

Following phrases accompany me during my meditation after the Pranayama practices:

- I breathe-in Your All sustaining Breath to enlighten my life with your Pranic Energy.
- I hold-breath to make me pure by holding Your Blessed Pranic Vibration in me.
- I breathe-out to make me empty, so that I can breathe again Your Pranic Energy.
- I wish that I can hold Your Breath for a while to have Your Presence with me, when I take my last journey to You.

Om Shivay nama   *Om Shivay nama*   *Om Shivay nama*

Glossary

ADYA-SHAKTI	:	Primal power or power of origin.
AFFERENT NEURONS	:	Peripheral sensory fibers carry neural signals toward the CNS, concerning the body's constantly changing status.
AHAM	:	Sanskrit word for self, I.
AIRWAYS	:	All conducting passageways of the respiratory tract.
AJNA	:	Name of the sixth Chakra.
AKASHA	:	Heavenly space, ether, space of higher intelligence.
ALVEOLUS	:	The regions of the lungs in which respiratory gas exchange (O_2 / CO_2) occurs.
ANAHATA	:	Name of the fourth Chakra.
ANULOMA	:	Name of a Pranayama practice.
APANA VAYU	:	In Yoga autonomous regulator of physiological function of excretion.
ASANAS	:	Third Discipline of Astanga Yoga, Physical postures.
ASTANGA YOGA	:	Eight disciplines of Yoga.
ATMAN	:	Immortal highest aspect of Brahma. The true self of pure consciousness, the last reality.
AUM	:	Creative word of cosmic vibration (Om). Well known mantra syllable.
AYAMA	:	Expansion in space and time
BANDHAS	:	Physical locks in Yoga system.
BHAKTI YOGA	:	Yoga of devotion.
BHASTRIKA	:	Name of a Pranayama practice.
BHRAMARI	:	Name of a Pranayama practice.
BIJA-MANTRA	:	Mystical sacred word that holds divine power, used in meditation.

BINDU	:	Point of metaphysical knowledge in Hindu scriptures, spiritual atom.
BRAHMA	:	The Hindu God in his aspect as creator, highest of the trinitarian supreme spirits.
BRAIN STEM	:	It is the stalk of brain, connecting the brain and spinal cord.
BREATH HOLDING	:	Voluntary cessation or absence of breathing movements, but not necessarily with a closed glottis.
BREATHING CYCLE	:	A ventilatory cycle consisting of an inspiration followed by the expiration of a volume of air.
BREATHING FREQUENCY	:	The number of breathing cycles per unit of time.
BREATHING MECHANISM	:	Movements of lung and thorax during each breathing cycle.
BREATHING PATTERNS	:	A general terms referring to the characteristics of the breathing activities.
CENTRAL NERVOUS SYSTEM (CNS)	:	A very complex system composed of the brain and spinal cord housing more than 100 billion neurons to organize and accomplish the functions of muscle activity, which are caused even by the most basic stimulus.
CHAKRA	:	Astral nerve center (anat. plexus).
CHANDRA BHEDA	:	Name of a Pranayama practice.
DHARANA	:	To conceive.
DHYANA	:	Meditation.
EFFERENT NEURONS	:	Motor fibers carry neural signals that are processed by CNS according to the information received through the sensory fibers to provide detail instructions to body's purposes, muscles.
EUPNEA	:	Normal spontaneous breathing pattern of which we are usually unaware. That is normal comfortable breathing at rest.
EXPIRATION	:	The process by which air is forced out of the lungs.
GUNA	:	Attitude, quality (philosophical view, Shvetashvatara-Upnishad).

HATHA YOGA	:	Yoga way of physical discipline with Prana control on the path of Raja Yoga.
HOMEOSTASIS	:	A tendency to stability in the normal body states (internal environment) of the organism.
HYPERPNEA	:	Increased breathing frequency to match increased metabolic demand.
HYPOTHALAMUS	:	A region in the brain, responsible for maintaining homeostasis.
ICCHA-SHAKTI	:	Will power.
IDA	:	Lunar astral nerve.
INSPIRATION	:	The active process that expands the lungs, allowing outside air to rush in.
JIVA	:	Individual soul, Human consciousness, perceiving and active spiritual monad.
JNANA SHAKTI	:	Power of knowledge.
JNANA YOGA	:	Yoga of knowledge.
KAPALABHATI	:	Name of a Pranayama practice.
KARMA YOGA	:	Yoga of selfless deeds.
KRIYA-SHAKTI	:	Handling power.
KRIYA YOGA	:	A process to realize the union of body and mind with the Atman at each form of activity of one's daily life.
KUMBHAKA	:	Breathholding in Yoga practice, after inspiration (Antara) or after expiration (Bajhya).
KUNDALINI	:	Coiled up snake.
KUNDALINI-SHAKTI	:	Sleeping cosmic power in man in form of sleeping coiled up snake.
KUNDALINI YOGA	:	Yoga of the dormant cosmic energy in human being. A branch of Raja Yoga.
LOTUS POSTURE	:	A posture of Yoga-Asana practice.
LUNG VOLUMES	:	A composition of eight subdivisions, see chapter I-2.
MAHESWAR	:	Another name of Hindu God Shiva, the destroyer, a trinity aspect of God.
MANIPURA	:	Name of the third Chakra.
MANTRA	:	Sacred word, mystical tonal energy.
MANTRA YOGA	:	A spiritual path of meditative singing or silent recitation of holy syllables (Mantra) of inherent divine power.

METABOLISM	:	The sum of all genetically determined chemical processes and associated energy transformations that occur within a living biologic system.
MUDRAS	:	Mystical formation of hands, gesture of eyes and so on.
MULADHARA	:	Name of the first Chakra.
MURCHHA	:	Name of a Pranayama Practice.
NADI	:	Sensory nerve of astral body.
NEURAL REGULATION	:	An active neural system that is capable of generating and maintaining a regular breathing cycle because respiratory muscles can not move alone.
NEURON	:	Individual nerve cells.
NIRGUNA	:	Without qualities, that lies beyond our approach.
NIRMANU	:	A physical method (Kriya).
NIYAMA	:	Rules and disciplines.
OM	:	Sacred mantra, symbol of Brahma. Its sound vibration encloses the key notes of all pervading existence. See also AUM.
PARAMAHANSA	:	Highest ascetic rank. Self-denying devotee.
PATANJALI	:	A philosopher (2nd century BC). The author of Yoga Sutra.
PERIPHERAL NERVOUS SYSTEM	:	Communication terminal for afferent and efferent signals.
PINGALA	:	Solar astral nerve.
PLAVINI	:	Name of a Pranayama practice.
PRAKRITI	:	Nature, highest principle of material world, matter of origin the initial manifestation of God.
PRAKRITI-SHAKTI	:	Power of nature.
PRANA	:	All sustaining life's energy. Cosmic manifestation of spiritual breath in living being.
PRANA VAYU	:	In Yoga autonomous regulator of physiological function of nervous system.
PRANAYAMA	:	A specific form of yogic breathing. The fourth discipline of Astanga Yoga. The central practice of Yoga.

PRATILOMA	:	Name of a Pranayama practice.
PRATYAHARA	:	Withdraw.
PURUSHA	:	Spiritual origin (Monade) of human being. The true light of human being (Brihad-Aranyaka-Upanishad).
RAJA-YOGA	:	King of Yoga arts. A Yoga science to reach absolute consciousness.
RAJAS GUNA	:	Passionate attitude.
RAM	:	A Bija mantra.
RESPIRATORY PHYSIOLOGY	:	A science dealing with the respiration process of a living body.
SAGUNA	:	With manifested qualities.
SAHASRARA	:	Name of the seventh Chakra.
SAMADHI	:	Union with the absolute in supreme consciousness.
SAMANA VAYU	:	In Yoga autonomous regulator of physiological function of digestion.
SAMANU	:	Name of a Pranayama practice.
SAMHITAS OR SANHITAS	:	Collection of hymns and verses from Vedas, used by priests for offer ceremonies.
SANKHYA	:	A philosophy, which itemizes the universal principle. Explains the origin of perception.
SASTRA	:	Scripture, book of laws theoretical science.
SATSANGA	:	Company of virtuous persons.
SATTVA GUNA	:	Positive attitude, pure nature.
SATYAM	:	Sanskrit word for truth.
SHAVASANA	:	A posture of Yoga-Asana practice (dead body posture).
SHAKTIPAT	:	Energy transfer from persons of higher energy level to others.
SHAKTISM	:	A metaphysical tenet of power.
SHATCHITANANDA	:	A word combination of *Sat, Chit, Ananda* means supreme bliss.
SHITAKARI	:	Name of a Pranayama Practice.
SHITALI	:	Name of a Pranayama Practice.
SHIVA-SHAKTI	:	Inseparable union of the reality and creating power. Another definition of Satchitananda. Sublimated physical union of men and women. Also interpreted as Purusha-Prakriti.

SHUKHASANA	:	A posture of Yoga-Asana practice.
SHUSHUMNA	:	Hollow Astral nerve.
SUFI	:	Mystic.
SUFISM	:	Mysticism of Islam.
SURYA BHEDA	:	Name of a Pranayama Practice.
SUTRA	:	Aphorism, Law, Rule of use.
SWADHISTHANA	:	Name of the second Chakra.
SWAMI	:	Title of an ascetic Hindu order.
TAM	:	A Bija mantra.
TAMAS GUNA	:	Attitude of darkness.
TANTRA	:	Sacred act of secret spiritual rituals.
TAT TVAM ASI	:	That are you.
THALAMUS	:	An important sensory integration center in brain.
THIRD EYE	:	In Sanskrit Trinayan, the place between the eye brows, the cradle place of inner vision, place of spiritual insight.
TIDAL VOLUME	:	Volume of air that is either inspired or expired during one breathing cycle, our normal breathing volume.
TRIPURASUNDARI	:	Manifestation of three gunas, symbolized by an equal sided triangle in chakra centers.
UDANA VAYU	:	In Yoga autonomous regulator of physiological function of cognitive skills, like speech and so on.
UJJAYI	:	Name of a Pranayama practice.
UPANISHAD	:	Secret teaching, Philosophical treaties. Approx. time period 750 to 550 BC.
VAYU	:	Sanskrit word for wind.
VEDA	:	The oldest scripture of Hindus (approx. 1500 BC), the eternal revelation.
VEDANTA	:	Designation for Upanishads that are composed at the end (anta) of the Vedic scriptures.
VILOMA	:	Name of a Pranayama practice.
VISHNU	:	Hindu God, the sustainer of creation, savior of universe, trinity aspect of supreme spirits.
VISHUDDHA	:	Name of the fifth Chakra.

VYANA VAYU	:	In Yoga autonomous regulator of physiological function of circulation.
YAM	:	A Bija mantra.
YAMA	:	All kinds of control.
YOGA	:	Verbally it means union. A specific method of contemplation to realize the spiritual unity between the higher self and the divine being through various disciplines.

Bibliography

CHOPRA, MD., Dr. DEEPAK: *"Ageless Body—Timeless Mind"* 1993, Harmony Books a division of Crown Publishers Inc. NY.

DHIRANANDA, YOGI: *"Yogamrita"*, German edition 1998, Veda Verlag, Wallmoden.

DEVANANDA, SWAMI VISHNU: *"Das grosse illustrierte Yoga-Buch"*, German edition 1989, Aurum Verlag GmbH & Co. KG, Freiburg im Breisgau; Original title: The complete illustrated book of Yoga, Bell Publishing Inc. NY.

ESOTERA: An esoteric German monthly magazine. Edition July and August, 1999, Freiburg.

GLASENAPP, HELMUTH v.: *"Die Philosophie der Inder"*, German edition 1949, Alfred Kroener Verlag, Stuttgart.

GLASENAPP, HELMUTH v.: *"Indische Geisteswelt"*, German edition 1958, Holle Verlag GmbH, Baden-Baden.

GREENWELL, Dr. PHIL. BONNIE: *"Kundalini"*, German edition 1998, Gustav Luebbe Verlag GmbH., Bergisch Gladbach. Original title *"Energies of Transformation, A Guide to the Kundalini Process"* 1990, USA.

IYENGAR, B.K.S.: *"Licht auf Pranayama"*, German edition 1992, Otto Wilhelm Barth Verlag, Munich. Original title "Light on Pranayama", George Allen & Unwin Ltd.

KHAN, HAZRAT INAYAT: *"The Sufi Message of Hazrat Inayat Khan"*, Barrie and Rockliff, London, 1960.

MUKHERJEE, Dr. G.S. & SPIEGELHOFF, Dr. W.: *"Yoga und unsere Medizin"*, German edition 1963, Hippokrates Verlag GmbH, Stuttgart.

NIKHILANANDA, SWAMI: *"Der Hinduismus"*, German edition 1958, Ullstein Taschenbuecher Verlag, Frankfurt am Main. Original title *"Hinduism, Its meaning for the liberation of the spirit"*, USA.

VIVEKANANDA, SWAMI: *"Raja Yoga"*, 1930, Advaita Ashrama, Mayavati, Almora, U.P., India.

YOGANANDA, PARAMAHANSA: *"Autobiographie eines Yogi"* German edition 1961, Otto Wilhelm Barth Verlag, Munich. Original title *"Autobiography of a Yogi"*, Self-Realization Fellowship. LA.

YUKTESWAR, SWAMI SRI: *"The Holy Science"* 1990, Self-Realization Fellowship. LA.

Index

cosmic 29
cosmic consciousness 30
cosmic energy 25

D

dharana 24
dhyana 24
diaphragm 3
digestion 41
disabilities 7
divine 25
duration of breath-hold 58
dynamics of breathing mechanism 47

E

earth 33
efferent impulse 14
ego 42
egos 20
emotion 31
emotional balance 107
ether 33
exhalation 48
expiratory reserve volume 3
external senses 21
extrathoracic 7

F

final relation 58
fire 33
fontanel 15
functional residual capacity 3

G

gunas 67, 104

H

ha 25
handling capacity 104

harmony 20
hatha-yoga 19
Hazrat Inayat Khan 33
healing capacity 40
healing potentials 39
Hildegard von Bingen 24
homeostasis 16
hyperventilation 5

I

Ida 101
inhalation 48
inspiratory Capacity 3
inspiratory reserve volume 3
interrupted respiration 75
intrathoracic pressure 7
involuntary nerves 41

J

jiva 100
jnana yoga 22

K

karma yoga 21
kriya yoga 19
kumbhaka 64
kundalini 13, 99
kundalini shakti 25
kundalini yoga 22
kundalini-shakti 100

L

larynx 7
life stream 24
lung capacity 2
lung volumes 2
lungs 44

science of physiology 49
sensory 21
sensory receptors 13
serpent power 101
sexuality vii
shaktipat 108
shaktism 99
Shiva 66
Shiva Swarodaya 95
Shiva-Shakti 100
shushumna 101
sitting modes 44
solar-plexus 39
soul 20
spinal chord 13
spinal column 45
spiritual 30
spiritual consciousness 32
spiritual ignorance 42
spiritual knowledge 42
spiritual union 19
Sri Ramakrishna 24
Sri Ramana Maharshi 24
Sri Swami Shivananda 22
Sri Yukteswar 30
swadhisthana 101
Swami Vishnu Devananda x
Swami Vivekananda x
swara yoga 95
sympathetic nervous system
    (SNS) 15, 49

T

tantrism 99
tat tvam asi 67
tha 25
tidal volume 3

timing relation 112
trachea 7
transcendental 66
turbinate 7

U

udana 41
upanishad 20, 30
upanishads 66

V

value of Pranayama 41
veda 66
vedas 29
ventilation rate 4
Vishnu 66
vishuddha 101
vision 15
vital 29
vital capacity 2
voluntary nerves 41
vyana 41

W

water 33
will power 104
withdraw 23

Y

yama 23
yoga vii
yoga asanas 19
yoga sutra 19
yoga sastra 19
yoga-breathing 39